SHROPSHIRE
STAFFORDSHIRE
RAILWAYS
Remembered

Leslie Oppitz

COUNTRYSIDE BOOKS

NEWBURY, BERKSHIRE

First Published 1993
© Leslie Oppitz 1993

COUNTRYSIDE BOOKS
3 CATHERINE ROAD
NEWBURY, BERKSHIRE

ISBN 1 85306 264 2

Produced through MRM Associates Ltd., Reading
Typeset by Acorn Bookwork, Salisbury
Printed in England

CONTENTS

BIBLIOGRAPHY

In compiling *Shropshire & Staffordshire Railways Remembered*, I have referred to numerous sources, many now out of print, which include the following and which can be recommended for further reading:

Author	Title	Publisher
Rex Christiansen	Forgotten Railways: Severn Valley and Welsh Border The West Midlands North and Mid Wales	David & Charles
Rex Christiansen	A Regional History of the Railways of Great Britain Vol 7 The West Midlands	David & Charles
Peter E Baughan	A Regional History of the Railways of Great Britain Vol 11 North and Mid Wales	David & Charles
R W Kidner	The Cambrian Railways	The Oakwood Press
Mike Lloyd	The Tanat Valley Light Railway	Wild Swan Publications Ltd
Eric S Tonks	The Shropshire & Montgomeryshire Railway	The Industrial Railway Society
Keith & Susan Turner	The Shropshire & Montgomeryshire Light Railway	David & Charles
Eric S Tonks	The Snailbeach District Railways	The Industrial Railway Society
Edward Griffith	The Bishop's Castle Railway	Edward Griffith
W Smith and K Beddoes	The Cleobury Mortimer and Ditton Priors Light Railway	Oxford Publishing Co
C R Lester	The Stoke to Market Drayton Line	The Oakwood Press
Allan C Baker	The Potteries Loop Line	Trent Valley Publications
R Keys and the NSR Society	The Churnet Valley Railway	Moorland Publishing Co
Allan C Baker	The Cheadle Railway	The Oakwood Press
Basil Jeuda	The Leek, Caldon & Waterhouses Railway	The North Staffordshire Railway Company
S C Jenkins	The Leek & Manifold Light Railway	The Oakwood Press
P Jones	The Stafford & Uttoxeter Railway	The Oakwood Press

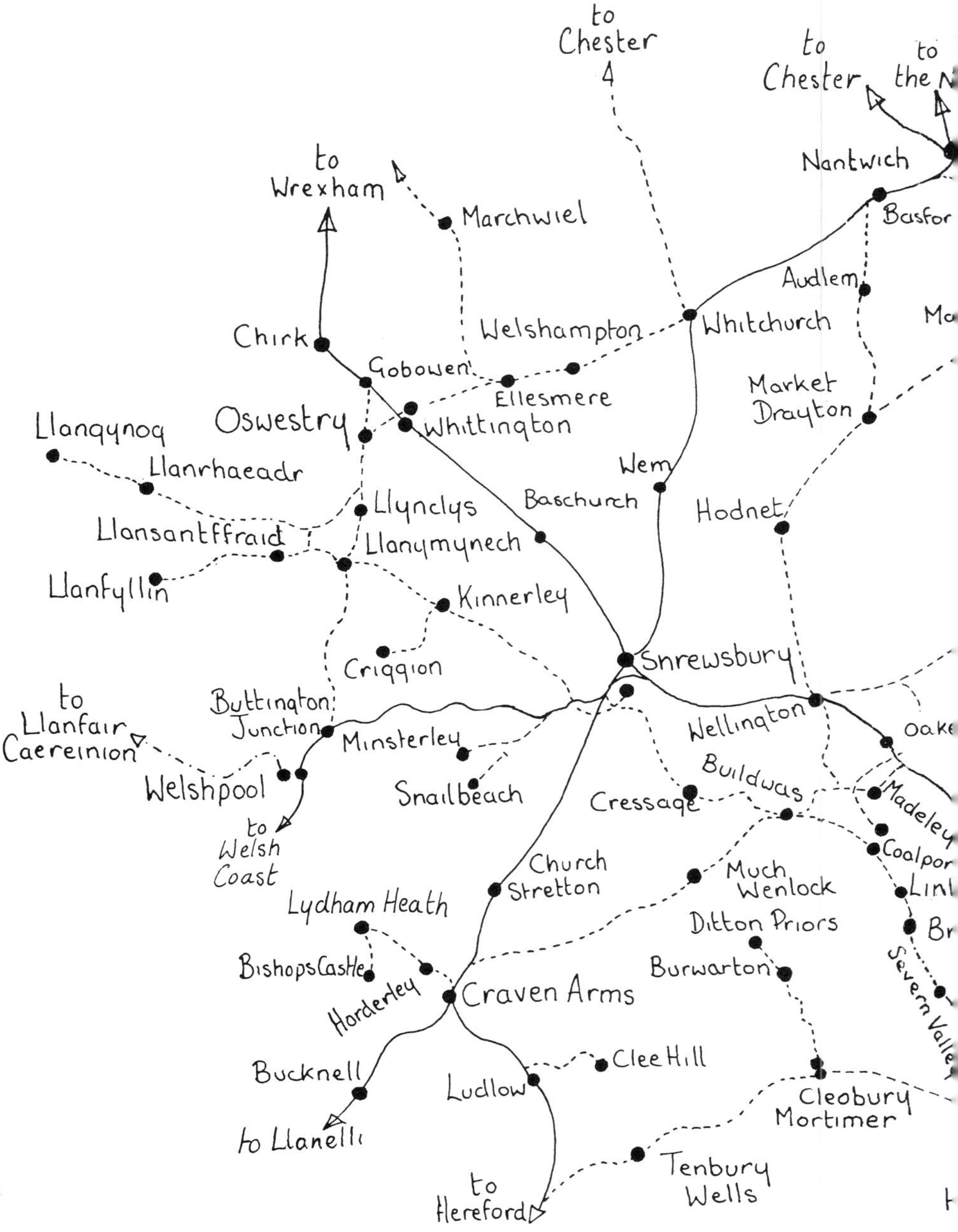

to Chester

to Chester

to the N

Nantwich

Basfor

to Wrexham

Marchwiel

Audlem

Welshampton

Whitchurch

Ma

Chirk

Gobowen

Market Drayton

Oswestry

Ellesmere

Whittington

Wem

Llangynog

Hodnet

Llanrhaeadr

Baschurch

Llynclys

Llansantffraid

Llanymynech

Llanfyllin

Kinnerley

Criggion

Shrewsbury

to Llanfair Caereinion

Buttington Junction

Minsterley

Wellington

Oake

Welshpool

Snailbeach

Buildwas

Madeley

Cressage

Coalpor

to Welsh Coast

Church Stretton

Much Wenlock

Linl

Lydham Heath

Ditton Priors

Br

BishopsCastle

Burwarton

Horderley

Craven Arms

Severn Valley

Bucknell

Clee Hill

Cleobury Mortimer

to Llanelli

Ludlow

to Hereford

Tenbury Wells

to Manchester

North Rode

Congleton

Wheelock

Rushton

Lawton

Biddulph

Hulme End

Leek

Endon

Thor's cave

Kidsgrove

Cheddleton

Waterhouses

dley Tunstall

Newcastle under Lyme

Bucknall

Caldon

Keele Stoke

Cheadle

Oakamoor

Ashbourne

Foxfield Railway

Cresswell

Alton

Trentham Park

Trentham

Rocester

Stone

Leigh

Uttoxeter

rton Bridge

Chartley

Tutbury

to Derby

nosall

Salt

Stafford

Burton-on-Trent

Rugeley

to Leicester

Wichnor

Cannock

Hednesford

Lichfield

to Wolverhampton

to Walsall

Brownhills

Tamworth

to Rugby

to Birmingham

to Birmingham

ey to Birmingham

Kidderminster

to Worcester

KEY
Lines in situ ————
Lines lifted or
closed to regular - - - - - - -
traffic
Preserved
railways —·—·—·—

ACKNOWLEDGEMENTS

Acknowledgements go to the numerous libraries and record offices throughout Shropshire and Staffordshire and many of the surrounding areas, who have delved into records and also to the staff at Oswestry library who never failed to locate an out-of-print book. Thanks also to J L Smith of Lens of Sutton and to D K Jones, John H Meredith, the Staffordshire County Museum at Shugborough, the City Central Library at Hanley, Cannock Library and the Borough Museum & Art Gallery at Newcastle-under-Lyme for their help in finding many old photographs.

Thanks also go to the following who generously contributed with information: William Jack of Market Drayton, Ken Lucas, Hon Secretary of the Bishop's Castle Railway Society, Paul Hughes, Publicity Officer of the Telford Horsehay Steam Trust Ltd., James Hutchinson, Chatterley Whitfield Museum Director, Gerard Burgess, British Rail Public Affairs, Birmingham, Mrs L J Reed, Hon Sec Foxfield Steam Railway and Richard Waterhouse, Director, North Staffordshire Railway Company (1978) Ltd.

Personal thanks go to Vernon Deadman and Nigel Oppitz for their help and finally sincere thanks to my wife, Joan, for travelling Shropshire and Staffordshire with me and also her careful checking of the final manuscript.

ABBREVIATIONS

BCR	Bishop's Castle Railway
CM&DPLR	Cleobury Mortimer & Ditton Priors Light Railway
GNR	Great Northern Railway
GVT	Glyn Valley Tramway Company
GWR	Great Western Railway
LMS	London, Midland & Scottish Railway
L&MVLR	Leek & Manifold Valley Light Railway
LNWR	London & North Western Railway
NSR	North Staffordshire Railway
OE&WR	Oswestry, Ellesmere & Whitchurch Railway
O&NR	Oswestry & Newtown Railway
S&BR	Shrewsbury & Birmingham Railway
SDR	Snailbeach District Railways
S&HR	Shrewsbury & Hereford Railway
S&MLR	Shropshire & Montgomeryshire Light Railway
SSR	South Staffordshire Railway
S&UR	Stafford & Uttoxeter Railway
SUR&CC	Shropshire Union Railways & Canal Company
SVR	Severn Valley Railway
S&W	Shrewsbury & Welshpool Railway
TVLR	Tanat Valley Light Railway
WM&CQR	Wrexham, Mold & Connah's Quay Railway
W&SJR	Wellington & Severn Junction Railway

INTRODUCTION

A steam locomotive hauling two coaches laden with passengers pulled slowly southwards out of Cheddleton station towards Uttoxeter on the Churnet Valley line. The engine was LMS class 4F no 442 built at Derby in October 1927. This was North Staffordshire Railway territory, a company affectionately known as 'Knotty' to its followers because of its use of the Staffordshire knot as its motif. But the train from Cheddleton did not reach Uttoxeter, travelling only a few hundred yards, and the date was 10th May 1992. The Victorian country station of Cheddleton closed to passengers nearly 30 years ago and the venue is currently the headquarters of the North Staffordshire Railway Company (1978) Ltd. Fortunately for the preservationists, track remains in situ along much of the former Churnet Valley route and there are hopes that at some future date steam trains from Cheddleton may reach Leek Brook to the north and Frogham to the south (see chapter 15).

Conventional railways as known today began in the 1820s, following George Stephenson's enthusiasm over locomotive engines. With the opening of the Stockton to Darlington Railway in 1825, the first steam train had arrived. Travelling was pretty uncomfortable in those early days with railway carriages beginning as stage-coach bodies attached to wagon bases. They were small, cramped, unlit and had no heating or travel facilities.

Trains first came to Staffordshire when the Grand Junction Railway opened between Birmingham and Warrington via Crewe on 4th July 1837. The line was of immediate benefit to the Potteries, with coaches offering services by road to and from such places as Whitmore and Madeley. It was a further ten years, December 1847, before the Trent Valley line opened from Rugby to Stafford, another strategically important main line but built to by-pass Birmingham and Wolverhampton. The North Staffordshire Railway soon followed, beginning modestly with a stretch from Stoke-on-Trent to Norton Bridge opening in April 1848 to link with the Stafford to Crewe main line. By the end of the year, the NSR had spread in many directions.

In Shropshire, Shrewsbury celebrated the arrival of trains from Chester on 12th October 1848. Shops were shut and church bells rang all day. In June 1849, trains from Shrewsbury reached Oakengates and a line opened from Wellington to Stafford. On 20th April 1852, the Shrewsbury & Hereford Railway reached Ludlow but again there were delays for the railway to be completed. Trains eventually arrived at Hereford from Shrewsbury in December 1853.

From these major routes, branch lines developed where steam trains made their way across open stretches of countryside, linking remote villages and towns. In numerous instances passenger traffic remained light throughout, although goods or mineral traffic provided essential services. Some lines suffered an early demise

9

simply because they became uneconomic and, with road transport fast competing, the Beeching cuts of the early 1960s also took their toll.

This book intends to examine the lives of the many 'lost' lines in the counties of Shropshire and Staffordshire as well as their decline and closure. It also includes the preserved lines and societies of today that are dedicated to keep the past alive. *Shropshire & Staffordshire Railways Remembered* provides the reader with a means to explore numerous closed stations that can be found and the many trackbeds that have survived, some converted to footpaths.

Chapter 1

CAMBRIAN RAILWAYS

(Whitchurch/Ellesmere/Oswestry, Ellesmere/Wrexham,
Oswestry/Llanymynech/Welshpool)

The Cambrian Railways came into being on 25th July 1864 when a number of smaller companies in Shropshire and North Wales amalgamated and established a headquarters at Welshpool. In 1866 the company decided to move its office and headquarters from Welshpool to Oswestry. Meantime a railway works had been built at Oswestry so that from the start the company used its own rolling stock and therefore carried out its own maintenance. As a result of the works, which cost £28,000 to build, Oswestry developed into an important railway centre and the town's population grew steadily.

Passenger services were slow to build up and opportunities were missed through Directors' disagreements. In 1884 a Receiver was appointed but this proved to be the company's saving for within a number of years the company was on a better footing. Tourist traffic slowly built up particularly to places such as Cardigan Bay and Barmouth, the latter fast becoming a boom town.

Whitchurch/Ellesmere/Oswestry
One of the companies that formed the Cambrian Railways was the Oswestry, Ellesmere & Whitchurch Railway (OE&WR) which had been planned as an important link between the London & North Western Railway's (LNWR) Shrewsbury-Crewe line and the

Ellesmere station was once a busy junction with trains to Oswestry, Whitchurch and Wrexham. Passenger services ended in January 1965. (Lens of Sutton)

Staff pose at Welshampton station c1910. Earlier in 1897 eleven people were killed in a serious accident at the station when an excursion train became derailed. (Lens of Sutton)

Frankton station c1910 between Ellesmere and Oswestry. The building survives today as a private residence, still retaining the Cambrian Railways coat of arms. (Lens of Sutton)

Welsh Coast.

Because of strong opposition from certain landowners, particularly east of Ellesmere, the company was forced to build its track across the swampy Fenn's Moss area. All efforts to drain the land proved fruitless and, in the end, the company sank a substantial raft of brushwood and timber to support the track. The section from Whitchurch to Ellesmere opened to goods traffic in April 1863 and passenger services began on 4th May. Completion of the Ellesmere-Oswestry section was delayed by further legal problems but eventually opened on 27th July 1864.

On 11th June 1897, disaster struck when an excursion on its return journey from mid Wales to Lancashire became derailed at Welshampton. Earlier that day a Cambrian Railways guard had complained that a small four-wheeled brake van was 'riding rough'. Despite this it was attached to the front of the excursion and Cambrian officials claimed at the subsequent inquest that it

12

was this vehicle which caused the crash. The inspecting officer thought differently, blaming the speed of the train over track which in the Welshampton area needed renewal. Eleven people died in the accident.

The line closed to passenger traffic in January 1965 but numerous reminders of the past still exist. Whittington High Level station has been completely demolished and the embankment on the east side of the existing 'live' line between Gobowen and Shrewsbury has given way to a modern housing estate. But Station House is still there, a private residence called 'High Level Station House', and the road has been named Cambrian Avenue. A scheme exists in 1992 to re-open Whittington (low-level) station on the Shrewsbury to Chester line, but difficulties exist over land needed for the station access.

Ellesmere/Wrexham

Numerous ideas were put forward for a line between Ellesmere and Wrexham during the latter part of the last century. The Manchester, Sheffield & Lincolnshire Railway worked with the Cambrian Railways towards an agreement with the Mid Wales Railway to provide an independent line between Birkenhead and the South Wales coalfields. Two links were required to complete the route. One was between Connah's Quay (near Queensferry) and Bidston on the river Mersey and the other was between Wrexham and Ellesmere.

The Wrexham Mold & Connah's Quay Railway (WM&CQR) opened in October 1888 but there were delays in building the section between Wrexham & Ellesmere. Parliament agreed the line in July 1885 but it was to be another ten years before services commenced. The first sod was cut on 11th July 1892 and the line was inspected in October 1895. There were three intermediate stations, Bangor-on-Dee, Overton-on-Dee and Marchwiel. The

Frankton station building is today a strictly private residence. The coat of arms on the facing wall reads 'Cambrian Railways Company 1864'. (Author)

Wrexham Central station still survives for services to Bidston. The track on the far right served trains to Ellesmere – the line closed in September 1962. (Lens of Sutton)

12½ mile branch was single and each station had two platforms with passing loops. New platforms and a footbridge were built at Wrexham (Central) station, originally the WM&CQR terminus.

Services began on 2nd November 1895 and the line was worked by the Cambrian Railways from the start. Cambrian trains were never worked beyond Wrexham Central station but this was no problem since connections were made with WM&CQR trains. Also the Central station was conveniently close to the town's shopping centre. Early locomotives were 4-4-0 side tanks and for many years the branch was a busy one.

In September 1896 a half-mile double-tracked loop was constructed to avoid a reverse at Ellesmere, so that trains could have a through run from Wrexham to Oswestry. It remained disused for a number of years but it re-opened in 1911 to provide a through service from Manchester via Wrexham to Aberystwyth. In 1914 halts were opened at Sesswick and Trench. During the First World War much of the traffic was diverted through Crewe but when the war ended the trains never returned.

When the Wrexham/Ellesmere branch was absorbed by the GWR in 1923 a further halt opened at Hightown. Others followed in the 1930s at Cloy, Elson and Pickhill. Such efforts to increase traffic did not prove successful and it was not until the Second World War that the line benefited when a Royal Ordnance Factory was built at Marchwiel. Passenger trains were suspended from 1940 to 1946 so that priority could be given to munitions traffic.

After the war, local industries replaced the munitions factory but, with road competition steadily increasing, the railway lost much of its use. Passenger services came to an end on 10th September 1962 but freight traffic survived many more years. When the twice-weekly china clay trains between Abenbury brickworks and Wrexham ceased in 1981, the line closed for good.

Today there are few reminders of the branch. Wrexham Central station still exists but only a single unstaffed platform remains. Older style second-class-only trains still make regular runs to

GWR 1400 class no 1416 at Oswestry on 16th September 1948. This locomotive, designed by C B Collett, was built in 1932. (John H. Meredith)

Bidston on the Wirral, making numerous stops and taking just under the hour. At Marchwiel the trackbed at the end of Station Road has become a walkway where a search in the undergrowth reveals traces of the former station. Abutments of the river Dee bridge at Bangor-on-Dee have survived although the station has gone. The former goods yard is a coal yard. Overton-on-Dee was sited well over a mile from the village and a sawmill covers much of the station area. At Ellesmere the former station area is an industrial site. The people of the town once had train services to Whitchurch, Oswestry and Wrexham but today the railway is no more.

Oswestry/Llanymynech/Welshpool
On 26th June 1855, Parliament approved plans submitted by the Oswestry & Newtown Railway (O&NR) for a line to be built between Oswestry and Welshpool. Just over two years later in August 1857, the ceremony of cutting the first sod was an opportunity for celebration. After the firing of guns at Powys Castle, a procession took place which included a wheelbarrow of solid mahogany carrying the company's crest, used by Lady Williams-Wynn for the occasion.

On 1st May 1860 passenger services commenced between Oswestry and Pool Quay. At Oswestry the line was joined by an existing 2½ miles of single track from Gobowen, opened in 1848, by the Shrewsbury & Chester Railway. Pool Quay to Welshpool followed on 14th August 1860 making possible an Oswestry to Welshpool service of six trains each way daily and two on Sundays. Doubling of the track was agreed by the Board of Trade in 1862 between Buttington and Welshpool and between Oswestry and Llanymynech in 1864. Buttington station opened with the Shrewsbury & Welshpool line in 1862 and at Llanymynech a platform was added in 1866 to serve the West Shropshire Mineral Railway (later known as the 'Potts' line – chapter 3).

Oswestry's first station served the line from Gobowen and the

Pant station looking towards Llanymynech not long before closure of the line in 1965. Today the platform and buildings have been completely demolished. (Lens of Sutton)

O&NR station was called Oswestry Cam. This situation lasted until 1924 when the first (GWR) station was abandoned and all traffic used the latter. The building is still there and, not far away, the original works can be reached by the footbridge which crosses the track. Single track exists today between Gobowen, Oswestry and Nantmawr Quarry. Unused since the late 1980s, the section, owned by Trainload Freight, is not redundant but 'mothballed' and there is a proposal in existence that it may be used to carry domestic waste to a possible site at Nantmawr.

Oswestry is also today the home of the Cambrian Railways Society, founded almost 20 years ago. Boxing Day 1991 was a proud occasion for the Society when it had three engines in steam for the first time. These were *Oliver Veltom* 0-4-0ST no 2131 built by Peckett & Sons Ltd in 1951, *Norma* 0-6-0ST Hunslet 3770 built 1952 and Beyer/Peacock no 1872 0-4-0ST built in 1879. The society's present aim is to extend to Middleton Road bridge (several hundred yards only) but hopes at some future date to use that existing single track to operate trains between Gobowen and Blodwell Junction. Much needs to be done before this can happen and enthusiasts can only hope the plans will prove successful.

To the south, a Cambrian Railways mineral branch to Porthywaen left the main line just before Llynclys station. This branch was subsequently used in 1904 when a line was built along the Tanat Valley to Llangynog (chapter 2). Llynclys station building has survived today having been attractively converted to a private residence. Next came Pant where all signs of the station have completely disappeared. The buildings and platform have gone and the adjacent canal has all but dried up. Only the name Station Road recalls the past.

Llanymynech was a busy junction. Apart from the through train services, trains also left for Shrewsbury via the Potts line (chapter 3) and also for Llanfyllin (chapter 2). Llanymynech station closed completely in January 1965 but if current planning goes ahead then this area, at present in industrial use, may become part of the

Llanymynech and Pant bypass scheduled for completion later in the 1990s.

After crossing the river Vyrnwy, trains reached Four Crosses (Llandysilio) station where today only the engine shed stands, lost among buildings on an industrial site. At Ardleen the station building and platform edge give evidence where trains once existed but at Pool Quay all signs have gone. Destruction of Pool Quay station gave road planners a chance to straighten out a short section of the adjacent A483.

After Buttington where tracks met those from Shrewsbury, Welshpool was not far distant. The 'French Renaissance' style Welshpool station building has survived but in mid 1992 the existing track (Shrewsbury/Welshpool/Newtown and beyond) was re-aligned to a single island platform just to the east and the original building has been put to private use.

Although outside the scope of this book, no visit to Welshpool would be complete without a visit to the narrow-gauge Welshpool & Llanfair Light Railway, originally opened in April 1903 and worked by the Cambrian Railways. Notable for its passage through the streets and alleys of Welshpool, the line closed to passengers in 1931 and to freight in 1956. Thanks to the splendid efforts of the Welshpool & Llanfair Light Railway Preservation Company, the line lives on today providing frequent daily services throughout much of the year.

Chapter 2

BRANCHES INTO WALES

(Llanymynech/Llanfyllin, Porthywaen/Blodwell Jct/Llangynog)

Llanymynech/Llanfyllin

Following the opening of the Oswestry & Newtown Railway (O&NR) from Oswestry to Welshpool in 1860, Llanfyllin, a market town set in the deep wooded valley of the river Cain in the Berwyn foothills, saw the opportunity for a rail link with Oswestry. A previous proposal for a narrow-gauge Llanfyllin & Llangynog Light Railway had been defeated, as was a West Midland Railway scheme to open a line through to the Welsh coast via Llanfyllin and by tunnelling through the Berwyns. Parliament approved the 8½ mile branch from Llanymynech to Llanfyllin on 17th May 1861. Submitted by the O&NR (part of Cambrian Railways from 1864), the branch opened on 17th July 1863 with through services to Oswestry.

A journey between Llanymynech and Llansantffraid, initially the only intermediate station on the branch, was not without its difficulties. At Llanymynech trains had to reverse from a north-end bay after which another reverse was necessary. This was due to the proximity of the Montgomeryshire Canal, so a shunting neck was constructed known as 'Rock Siding'. Further stations on the branch followed in 1866 at Llanfechain and Bryngwyn. The latter was at first a 'flag stop' since, on Tuesdays and Wednesdays only, intending passengers had to work a signal on the platform to stop trains. It was later raised to the status of station.

The Llanfyllin Railway had a rather unexciting existence for most of its life even though it lasted for over a century. From 1881 Llanfyllin acquired importance as a railhead when large quantities of equipment arrived for the construction of Liverpool Corporation's Vyrnwy Reservoir scheme. Vast amounts of cement and iron pipework were delivered from Aberdovey Harbour on the Cardigan Bay coast. In January 1896 the reversal problem at Llanymynech was overcome when a ½ mile curve was opened, allowing a direct approach to the branch by using a section of the original Potteries, Shrewsbury & North Wales line. In 1938 Carreghofa Halt was opened on this stretch.

From 1936 GWR class 74XX 0-6-0PT locomotives were introduced. Previously an 0-4-2T, introduced by the GWR for light branches, had been a frequent sight along the Cain valley usually hauling a Swindon built twin set comprising two non-corridor brake coaches. The last steam train to work the line was hauled by Ivatt-designed BR class 2 locomotive no 46506. As it passed Llanymynech the name board still claimed for main line travellers, 'Change for Llanfyllin and Lake Vyrnwy'. Nothing was said about

the walk of more than eight miles that was necessary for the latter!

At Llanfyllin the terminus was quite substantial. Dominated by a large Victorian building (still in use today by an industrial company), it had a single platform with a run-round loop and a large yard with numerous buildings. A large part of the goods traffic comprised sheep and lambs. Freight traffic came to an end on the Llanfyllin branch in 1964 with all traffic ceasing from 18th January 1965, the same day that Whitchurch to Welshpool services terminated. With so little traffic on these lines, they could hardly be expected to be spared.

Llansantffraid station building lives on as the popular Station Restaurant. Opened in 1968, three years after closure of the line, extensive alterations have been made. Today customers can still savour the atmosphere of the old station, sitting where once passengers waited perhaps for a train to Oswestry to do their

Llansantffraid in Cambrian Railways days when six trains called each way on weekdays. The building is today 'The Station Restaurant'. (Lens of Sutton)

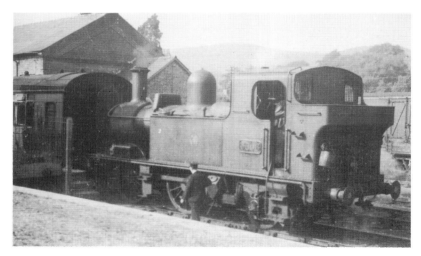

GWR 0-4-2T at Llanfyllin in the 1940s. The railway company claimed, 'Change at Llanfyllin for Lake Vyrnwy' not mentioning that a walk of more than eight miles was needed! (Lens of Sutton)

shopping. In the restaurant many pictures of the branch recall the past, timetables are preserved and even the station clock is on show. The restaurant is a must for train enthusiasts and non-enthusiasts alike.

Porthywaen/Blodwell Jct/Llangynog

The attractive village of Llangynog at the foot of the Berwyns came into prominence with the development of lead and slate working in the area. Lead mines on Craig Rhiwarth were discovered in 1692 and in the early 18th century a vein of almost pure galena (a source of lead ore) was found. As transport improved in the mid-19th century, Llangynog came close to prominence once again when a railway was planned in 1860 putting the village on the through route of a proposed West Midlands, Shrewsbury & Coast of Wales Railway. To proceed it was necessary to tunnel through the Berwyns but, when the high cost to achieve this was realised, the idea was dropped.

With Llangynog's mining activities hampered by the need for adequate transport to carry the ores to the smelting works (one was at Pool Quay), inevitably numerous ideas for branch lines followed but it was to be many more years before such a proposal was achieved. It took the Light Railway Act of 1896 to expedite matters and by the following year two plans were being considered. Firstly a proposal came from the Llanfyllin & Llangynog Light Railway for a 2 ft 6 in gauge line to be built from the Cambrian Railways terminus at Llanfyllin. The other came from the Tanat Valley Light Railway (TVLR) for a standard gauge line to link Llangynog with the existing Porthwaen mineral branch. The Porthywaen branch had opened in 1861 to serve limestone quarries and ran from Porthywaen junction on the Cambrian Railways main line.

Local feeling favoured the standard gauge line. It was considered this would not only provide an adequate outlet for the quarries but cater for people travelling to Oswestry for the market

Llanfyllin station in the 1940s. The 8½ mile branch from Llanymynech closed in January 1965 with the terminus becoming an industrial site. The platform building has survived. (Lens of Sutton)

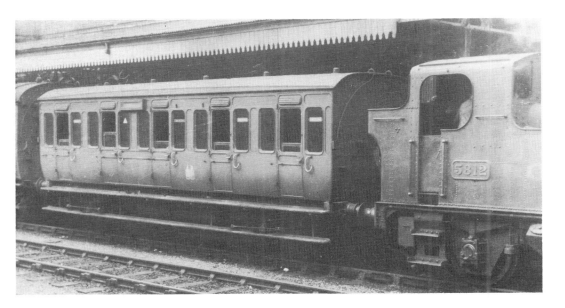

or for shopping. In addition trains could carry further pipes needed at the Vyrnwy Reservoir. The Board of Trade confirmed a Light Railway Order for the standard gauge Tanat Valley Railway on 4th January 1899.

A Tanat Valley branch train at Oswestry in September 1948. GWR 0-4-2T 1400 class no 5812 hauls a passenger set including 4-wheeled coach no 15. (John H. Meredith)

The ceremony of cutting the first sod took place on 12th September 1899 in a large field at Porthywaen where a grandstand covered with bunting had been erected. Close by stood a big marquee 'bulging with food for the luncheon to follow', an event that a local newspaper later described as 'the jolliest bun-fight seen in the area for many a year'.

Construction of the line went ahead but there were many problems. Apart from the perhaps predictable bad weather, the contractor made slow progress. There was an occasion when the directors paid an unexpected visit to the sites to find them deserted and the navvies sacked. To make up lost time, work was continued on Sundays, this bringing complaints from those 'grateful for the Sabbath'. Finance too was a problem and further assistance came from the Treasury and local councils and also Liverpool Corporation with its interest in the Lake Vyrnwy reservoir.

At the formal opening of the TVLR on 5th January 1904, the Dowager Lady Williams Wynn performed the ceremony at Porthywaen where level crossing gates were closed across the track secured by a silver chain and padlock. Lady Williams Wynn opened the railway by unlocking the padlock with a gold key and the train, Cambrian four-wheeled coaches hauled by a Seaham class 2-4-0, left for Llangynog.

Public and goods services began the next day. The branch, worked by the Cambrian Railways, consisted of ten intermediate stations with Porthywaen Junction being renamed Llynclys Junction. A weekdays only service provided four trains daily between Oswestry and Llangynog. It was not long however before the

A 1910 view of Llanrhaeadr-ym-Mochnant station on the Llangynog (Tanat Valley) branch. The station became the railhead in the early 1950s when traffic in coal and agricultural products provided the only source of income. (Lens of Sutton)

TVLR ran into trouble. The costs of construction had proved to be double those of the original estimate and it was soon realised that traffic would not reach the levels expected. Within three months a Receiver was appointed, a situation that was to remain until the Cambrian Railways took over the line in March 1921. The following year the Cambrian Railways formally became part of the GWR.

For many years the TVLR continued undisturbed along the quiet valleys. Track maintenance on the single-track branch was often neglected. More than once the leading wheels of the Seaham tank locomotives dropped between the rails where the track had spread and a crowbar had to be carried to ease the wheels back on to the rails. The most important intermediate station was at Llanrhaeadr-ym-Mochnant which possessed a crossing loop, two platforms and a platform building which included the luxury of a separate ladies' WC tacked on to the booking office/waiting room! In later years as stone traffic ceased, Llanrhaeadr served as a railhead in coal, lime, fertilisers and animal feedstuffs.

During the Second World War, the TVLR reduced its passenger services but they were not increased again when the war ended. When a national coal shortage came in 1951 all services were 'withdrawn temporarily' but they were never to return. Passenger services ceased officially on 5th February 1951 to be replaced by road services operated by Crosville Motor Services Ltd. In July 1952 freight services were withdrawn between Llangynog and Llanrhaeadr and for a time the stretch of track accommodated withdrawn wagons. In December 1960, following damage to a bridge caused by floodwater, the line between Llanrhaeadr and Blodwell Junction closed completely.

Today sections of the trackbed can be traced although nearly all the stations have vanished. At Llangynog a short section of platform has survived in a caravan park. When the line closed there seemed possibilities for preservation but alas this was not to be. The TVLR, poor throughout its existence, never achieved the importance of its neighbouring Llanfyllin branch.

Chapter 3

THE 'POTTS' LINE

(Shrewsbury/Kinnerley/Llanymynech, Kinnerley/Criggion)

A mile to the south of Kinnerley a bridge crosses where a railway junction once served the local folk, providing trains to Shrewsbury, Llanymynech or even Criggion. The trains have long since gone but the memories remain, for those were the days of the Shropshire & Montgomeryshire Railway, or the 'Potts' line as it became known. There were engines with such names as *Pyramus, Hesperus, Thisbe, Daphne* and *Dido*. Another, still remembered by many today was *Gazelle*, nicknamed the *Coffee Pot*. It was built at Kings Lynn in 1893 and brought to the Potts line in 1911.

The railway had a complex and undulating history. Its future could hardly have been considered prosperous since it covered an area of scattered farmlands and small villages as well as crossing ground subject to periodic heavy flooding. Planned originally as the West Shropshire Mineral Railway between Westbury and Llanymynech, it was succeeded by the Shrewsbury & North Wales Railway which proposed to leave the Welshpool line at Redhill plus a three mile extension from Llanymynech to Llanyblodwel to serve the Nantmawr lime kilns. At Kinnerley a six mile branch was planned to the granite quarries at Criggion.

The proposals became reality when the North Staffordshire Railway backed the venture thus creating the Potteries, Shrewsbury & North Wales Railway – hence the nickname, the 'Potts'. It was also intended to carry passengers. However plans to seek running powers over the existing main line into Shrewsbury General station were turned down by Parliament, so an independent approach had to be made with the building of Abbey Foregate station. The terminus was sited where the former Abbey Refectory

Kinnerley station, looking towards Llanymynech. The bay platform on the far left was for Criggion trains but more often than not it accommodated idle, crippled or life-expired vehicles. (Lens of Sutton)

once stood, with the pulpit (built late 14th century) remaining railed-off in the station yard and scheduled as an ancient monument.

When the line first opened on Monday, 13th August 1866, providing passenger services on double track between Shrewsbury and Llanymynech, no official ceremony took place. Yet the local people were not prepared to let such an occasion pass without note. According to *The Shrewsbury Chronicle*, large numbers of passengers from Shrewsbury arrived at Llanymynech in special excursion trains where they either 'ascended Llanymynech Hill' or 'sought sport in the river Vyrnwy as well filled baskets testified'.

All did not go well, for the company soon ran into financial difficulties. It struggled on until 3rd December 1866 when the bailiffs moved in. In their book, *The Shropshire & Montgomeryshire Light Railway*, Keith and Susan Turner wrote of an amusing tale of when a debenture holder obtained a writ against the company. A train arriving at Abbey Foregate was seized but after much haggling it was allowed to leave with a bailiff on board. He was duly settled in a first-class compartment but on arrival at Llanymynech he was politely moved to a compartment set aside for him.

After calling at Kinnerley on the return journey, there was a short period of shunting. As the train left for Shrewsbury, the bailiff became suspicious and, looking out of the window, he saw the rest of the train disappearing into the distance. Arriving rather footsore at Shrewsbury after midnight, he was informed that a coupling chain had broken and his coach had been left behind – quite by accident!

Finances remained a problem, so traffic was suspended on 21st

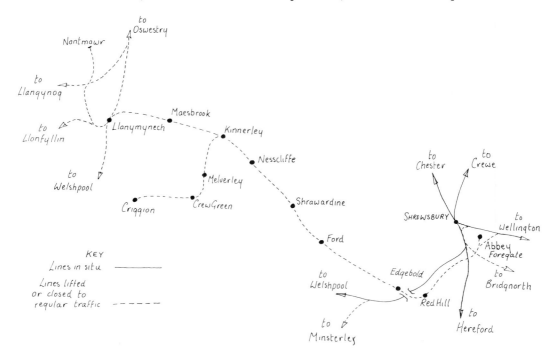

24

December 1866 until some of the company's assets could be realised. A plan was considered to amalgamate with a number of small Welsh railway companies but this was rejected. Another idea was to build a spur from Abbey Foregate station to connect with a proposed Market Drayton link but again this did not happen.

Eventually in December 1868, services were resumed but they were at a reduced level and the line had been singled. In 1871 a branch opened from Kinnerley to Criggion, mainly for freight traffic although there was some passenger traffic. Except for Melverley's brick structure, the few stations on the branch were initially wooden buildings and a viaduct across the river Severn was described as rickety. The company benefited from additional freight traffic when a year later in 1872 a further branch extended beyond Llanymynech to Nantmawr where ample limestone could

The 'Potts' line was not allowed access to Shrewsbury's main station so a terminus was built at Abbey Foregate. LMS (ex-LNWR) locomotive 0-6-0 no 8108 waits to leave for Llanymynech in the early 1930s. (Lens of Sutton)

A lone passenger at Crew Green station on the branch to Criggion. The platform was equipped solely with a former tramcar seat taken from the tram brought by Col. Stephens for use on the branch. This view is taken looking towards Melverley in 1937. (Lens of Sutton)

25

be found. To reach Nantmawr, the company had to obtain agreement with the Cambrian Railway company for running powers over their metals at Llanymynech.

Matters overall did not improve and finances continued to deteriorate. All possible economies were made and fares were reduced. In 1877 an Official Receiver was appointed and in 1880 a 25 mph speed limit was imposed until the standard of the track was improved. This never happened and services were further cut back and later in 1880 all traffic was again suspended.

In 1881 the Cambrian Railway took over the line west of Llanymynech with this short section re-opening in 1886. A new company called Shropshire Railways emerged in 1890 and the track between Llanymynech and Shrewsbury was relaid. Once again receivership followed and the buildings and other structures went into further decay. In 1902, the 'rickety' wooden viaduct over the Severn at Melverley collapsed.

Local pressure to re-open the line came in 1907 and the Shropshire & Montgomeryshire Light Railway (S&MLR) was formed, largely financed by local councils. A Light Railway Order was issued in February 1909 and work began to clear the track, all the sleepers were replaced and Melverley Viaduct was rebuilt. The engineer was H F Stephens, later Colonel Stephens, well known for his light railway adventures elsewhere in the country. The line re-opened on Maundy Thursday, 13th April 1911, when the Mayor of Shrewsbury, Major Wingfield, gave an opening speech from the top of a freshly painted ex-Midland Railway coach to a large crowd. Later an eight-coach special, hauled by 0-6-0 ex-LSWR *Hesperus*, left for Llanymynech amidst exploding detonators and loud cheering.

Over the next twenty years traffic remained at a low level, hardly surprising for such a thinly populated area with rural halts miles from anywhere. The Criggion branch re-opened in February 1912 for freight and for passengers six months later. Sometimes trains from Shrewsbury were used by walkers or parties who wished to visit the surrounding countryside at Llanymynech or the Breidden Hills at Criggion.

In the 1920s, economies on the Potts line included experiments with Ford railcars although these proved somewhat unpopular. They became known as 'The Rattlers' leaving passengers with a ringing in their ears from the noise created by the pressed steel wheels. An unusual vehicle purchased by Colonel Stephens and converted for use with *Gazelle* was a double-deck tramcar originally drawn by two horses in London.

When Colonel Stephens died in 1931 the line further deteriorated. In the following years passenger trains on the Criggion branch ceased beyond Melverley, since the viaduct was once again considered unsafe. In November 1933 all regular S&MLR passenger services ceased and only excursions survived. Gradually stations decayed and the weeds took over the track once again. Yet despite its apparent end, the line was to experience yet another lease of life.

In June 1941 the section from Shrewsbury to Llanymynech was requisitioned by the War Department (WD) to serve the extensive ammunition depots which had been established throughout the area. Kinnerley yard became rife with khaki and the sidings were full of military stock. Nissen huts sprang up like mushrooms and yet again the line was relaid, this time with concrete sleepers. Soon as many as twelve locomotives were in steam simultaneously. Numerous sidings served over 200 ammunition store buildings, the system worked by the No 1 Group of the Royal Engineers.

Towards the end of the war it became necessary to rebuild the up side of a viaduct at Shrawardine where a pillar showed distinct signs of sagging. Royal Engineer personnel cut down the original girders and a bailey bridge structure able to take heavier loads was placed on the remaining pillars. Shortly after the war, floods in the area were worse than usual with water reaching the top of the embankment at Shrawardine. At the same time a bridge over a stream at Maesbrook was completely swept away, stranding a locomotive at Llanymynech.

In 1959 the WD closed its last depot and in the same year the stone traffic from Criggion ceased. In 1960 the line returned to civilian status and operations were gradually run down. The last scheduled train ran from Shrewsbury to Llanymynech on 26th February 1960 and on 29th February the line closed officially. A farewell trip took place in March by the Stephenson Locomotive Society. Shrawardine viaduct was dismantled in 1962 but Melverley viaduct on the already closed Criggion branch was rebuilt as a road bridge. In the same year BR completed removal of all track apart from oil depot sidings at Shrewsbury which had been connected to British Rail tracks in 1960.

The 'Potts' line had at last been laid to rest but many today recall the days of steam with affection. At Kinnerley the magic is still there. The platform building has survived although overgrown

Maesbrook station during the Second World War when the line was used by the War Department to serve munition depots. (Lens of Sutton)

The locomotive Gazelle used on the 'Potts' line was nicknamed The Coffee Pot. Picture taken at Kinnerley shed. (Lens of Sutton)

with trees and shrubs. Along the line towards Criggion, the Kinnerley shed which was refurbished by the WD in July 1941 is today in industrial use and the water tower, erected in 1958 to replace an earlier one, still stands close by. The locomotive *Gazelle* can be found at the Museum of Army Transport at Beverley in North Humberside. It is there on long-term loan from the National Railway Museum and forms part of the permanent display. It is still in good condition visually but if ever it were to be steamed again it would need a new boiler.

A local from Maesbrook recalled a tale from his grandmother's days. Whilst travelling on the Potts line, the train, which ran slowly enough at the best of times, suddenly juddered to a halt. She leaned out of the window and shouted to the driver, 'What's up?' 'Sheep on the line', came the reply. In a short while the train started again and then once more shuddered to a halt. 'What's up this time?' shouted the impatient passenger. 'We've caught up the sheep', came the driver's terse reply.

After a while the driver shouted back, 'Why don't you get out and walk – it could be quicker'. 'I can't do that' she replied, 'I'm being met at the station and I said I'd be on this train. . .'

Chapter 4

A JOINT LINE TO MINSTERLEY AND A MINERAL BRANCH

(Shrewsbury/Pontesbury/Minsterley, Pontesbury/Snailbeach)

Shrewsbury/Pontesbury/Minsterley

A 9½ mile branch from Shrewsbury to Minsterley opened on 14th February 1861 with intermediate stations at Hanwood, Plealey Road and Pontesbury. The section from Shrewsbury to Cruck-meole junction later became part of the Shrewsbury to Welshpool (S&W) line which opened on 27th January 1862, joining the Oswestry & Newtown Railway at Buttington. The Minsterley branch remained single throughout its life even though bridges on the S&W section allowed for later possible doubling.

On 5th July 1865 the S&W and Minsterley branches became vested in the LNWR and the GWR jointly. Passenger traffic to Minsterley was never heavy with four trains daily each way but none on Sundays. By the turn of the century this had improved to seven daily and one Sunday train each way. The journey took just over half an hour taking passengers along the attractive Rea Brook valley and skirting Pontesford Hill. Apart from passenger services, the branch also attracted milk and agricultural traffic but it was the mineral traffic which came down from the Stiperstones on the Snailbeach District Railways to an exchange point at Pontesbury that kept the line profitable. The mines in turn created a need for coal.

From April 1919 competition for passengers came from a bus service which began between Minsterley and Shrewsbury. The railway countered with various offers including through market tickets and, for a time, it held its own. As an economy measure,

In February 1861 the Shrewsbury & Welshpool Railway opened a branch to Minsterley hoping to benefit from the lucrative quarry traffic from the nearby Stiperstones. Today the sawmills have gone, replaced by a yoghurt factory. (Lens of Sutton)

Pontesbury was an important intermediate station on the Minsterley branch. Here Station House survives and the former goods shed to the right of the picture is today the HQ of the Pontesbury Gardeners' Association. (Author)

trains from Minsterley were mixed freight and passenger. After grouping in 1922, the branch became GWR & LMS Joint and it was a familiar sight to see LMS (ex-LNWR) 0-6-2 coal tanks along the line. During the Second World War, passenger services enjoyed a new lease of life because petrol shortages meant that rural buses had to cut back.

The Minsterley branch finally fell victim to road competition with its closure to passenger traffic on 5th February 1951. The closure also came at a time when the country was suffering a coal crisis. Freight traffic survived another 16 years, until May 1967, and the track was finally lifted in 1973. The line from Shrewsbury to Welshpool still exists of course, although Hanwood station, initially an intermediate station on the Minsterley branch, closed to passengers in 1960 when all the intermediate stations and halts on the S&W were closed.

It is not difficult to trace the Minsterley branch. At Plealey Road the level crossing has gone but the station building is still there as a private residence. Similarly Pontesbury station building has become 'Station House' and a short awning that once covered a section of the platform can be seen from Station Road. The nearby goods shed is used by the Pontesbury Gardeners' Association.

At one time the terminus at Minsterley boasted a milk wharf, a goods shed, cattle and horse docks and numerous sidings. During a visit in April 1992, the author found a local resident who recalled the GWR/LMS days. Starting work at Shrewsbury in 1927 as a parcel porter, he was transferred to Minsterley after the Second World War in 1947 as a freight checker where he remained until closure. Station House has survived but little else. Today a private residence, the owner Harold Bradley (known locally as 'Brad') recalled the trouble he had removing the concrete base that had previously supported a water tower. 'It was four feet thick and needed a lot of hard work to remove it' he reflected, 'When they did things in those days, they did them properly!'

Pontesbury/Snailbeach

It is known that mining existed at the Stiperstones centuries ago when the Romans obtained lead from shallow borings and their old workings can still be traced in the Hope district. Mining was not taken seriously in the area until the 19th century when a small number of moderately sized concerns came into existence. As business grew, so transport increased as a problem. Various schemes were put forward to run trains along the Rea valley but it was not until the branch from Shrewsbury opened on 14th February 1861 that rail transport became available. Even so, this only reached as far as Minsterley which was still some distance from the mines themselves.

It was because of this that the Snailbeach District Railways (SDR) later came into existence. The company was incorporated by an Act of Parliament dated 5th August 1873 which authorised two railways each of 2 ft 4 in gauge. The first was planned to run westwards from Pontesbury station (on the Minsterley branch) to Crowsnest, just beyond Snailbeach village. The second line was to be an extension of just under two miles skirting the Stiperstones to reach lead mines at Pennerley. Finance proved difficult to attract, particularly since this was not intended to be a passenger carrying railway, and only the first railway was built.

The village of Snailbeach today owes much of its existence to the days of mining. Many of the dwellings go back to these earlier times as do their local places of worship, the public houses (some now private properties) and two schools (one has become a Field Centre). The miners were great sports enthusiasts, marbles contests were regularly held and footballers were renowned for their robust play. Choirs were notable with a popular slogan being, 'Sing

Trains on the 2 ft 4 in gauge Snailbeach District Railway reached Crowsnest and then reversed up the side of the hill to the mines. (Lens of Sutton)

31

for lead, whistle for coal'.

When the narrow gauge Snailbeach District Railways (SDR) opened in 1877, its future seemed prosperous. The annual tonnage carried in the first five years averaged at 14,000 tons and shareholders benefited from a 3% dividend. Some 40 wagons were in use, hauled initially by 0-4-2ST *Belmont*, assisted later by 0-6-0ST *Fernhill*, delivered in 1881. The company's good fortune was not to last, for in 1884 the SDR suffered when one of its best customers, the Tankerville Great Consuls Company, closed its mines in Tankerville, Pennerley and The Bog. This had the effect of reducing the annual tonnage to around 5,500 annually.

The SDR seemed doomed to extinction but relief came when the Ceiriog Granite Company opened a quarry in 1905 on the north side of Eastridge Wood, near Habberley. A branch line was built to the quarry and during the following year over 20,000 tons of mineral traffic were carried. Extra power was needed and the Glyn Valley Tramway Company (GVT) made available *Sir Theodore*, a 0-6-0T built by Beyer Peacock. Unfortunately the GVT gauge was 2 ft 4½ in and the flanges of *Sir Theodore* kept riding up the sides of the Snailbeach metals so the engine had to be returned. A new locomotive was supplied in 1906, a six coupled side tank with the name of *Dennis*.

Locomotive WD538 no 3, rebuilt and regauged from 1 ft 11½ ins to 2 ft 4 ins by Bagnall in 1918, photographed at Snailbeach on 15th September 1948. (John H. Meredith)

By 1909 the annual tonnage reached 38,000 but this state of affairs was not to last and trade fell off once more. The First World War (1914–1918) further worsened the situation and trade continued to dwindle. Help came once again in 1923 when Colonel Stephens, a man renowned for his light railway exploits throughout the country, took over. Efficiency improved at once and, although lead traffic had virtually disappeared, a barytes mine had opened

Happily for posterity the Snailbeach locomotive shed still exists having been recently refurbished through the auspices of Shropshire County Council. Not far away sections of track and points with their levers have survived the 33 years since closure. (Author)

with a new quarry on Callow Hill.

In the book *The Snailbeach District Railways*, Eric S Tonks wrote of the period in the 1920s when the line was almost entirely worked by a driver-cum-fitter by the name of Gatford who had served earlier on the Bishop's Castle Railway. Driver Gatford ran the SDR virtually single-handed, keeping the engines and wagons in working order with the limited resources available. At least he had no commuting problems. At the end of each day he would leave the engine, after taking on coal and water, on the track outside his garden gate ready for the next day's work.

Colonel Stephens died in 1931 and by the following year the SDR was entirely dependent on the quarry at Callow Hill for traffic. Three further locomotives were purchased and, under new management, quarrying continued. The SDR survived until 1947 when Shropshire County Council, lessees of the Callow Hill quarries, purchased the line. Traffic struggled on until 1959 when the last available locomotive failed and for a time a diesel farm tractor straddled the rails to haul wagons.

A visit to Snailbeach today can prove most rewarding. Located to the south of Minsterley and off the A488, a narrow road climbs to cross the redundant trackbed by a chapel. At a higher point a rough turning leads off to the left where once existed numerous mines and it is here that the locomotive shed, recently refurbished by Shropshire County Council, can be found.

Chapter 5

BISHOP'S CASTLE RAILWAY

(Craven Arms/Stretford Bridge/Lydham Heath, Lydham Heath/
Bishop's Castle)

The townsfolk of Bishop's Castle had long wanted a railway link with 'the outside world'. Plans were deposited in 1860 and the whole route was surveyed. There was however much dissatisfaction when it was learned that the initial proposal gave priority to a line linking the Oswestry & Newtown Railway at Montgomery with the Shrewsbury & Hereford Railway (S&HR) at Wistanstow to the north of Craven Arms, at the same time shelving the idea of a branch to their own town.

When the public were invited to buy shares in the Bishop's Castle Railway (BCR), the *Shrewsbury Chronicle* of 22nd March 1861 commented, 'The railway is a misnomer, for Bishop's Castle will never enjoy much, if any, of its vast benefits'. As a result of local feeling, the Committee of the House of Commons introduced a clause in the Railway Bill ensuring that a branch from Lydham Heath to Bishop's Castle must be opened concurrently with the main branch.

A proposal was also under consideration from the competing Shrewsbury & Welshpool Railway to extend its newly-opened Minsterley branch through Chirbury to Bishop's Castle providing a direct link with Shrewsbury. This latter plan received considerable backing from numerous tradespeople who travelled to London to give their support. Unfortunately their journey was undertaken before consultation with several local prominent people (including a clergyman) who preferred the original Bishop's Castle Railway proposals. As a result these same gentlemen immediately closed their accounts with the tradespeople concerned and the clergyman even asked that they should be excluded from his church!

Despite this opposing scheme, the Bishop's Castle Railway Bill received Royal Assent on 28th June 1861 agreeing a line from Montgomery to Wistanstow, plus a branch from Lydham Heath (requiring a reversal) to Bishop's Castle, giving a total length of 19¼ miles. Final surveys and working plans were completed during 1862 and negotiations to acquire the necessary land were put in hand. The junction with the Shrewsbury & Hereford Railway was meantime changed from Wistanstow to Stretford Bridge.

Work by the contractor, Mr Savin, started in March 1863 but it was not long before there were serious delays. Apart from the lack of available finance, the BCR also had grave misgivings over Mr Savin. His company was clearly overstretching itself, with additional involvements in construction work on the Cambrian

Railways as well as the building of numerous hotels. A bill was filed in Chancery by the BCR to recover the sum of £20,500 already advanced and a new contractor, Mr G M Morris of Plowden, was appointed. Many had given up hope that the line would ever be built. Work eventually started on 24th October 1864 on the Lydham Heath to Bishop's Castle section and the town celebrated that night with the ringing of church-bells and a bonfire.

Staff pose proudly in front of ex-GWR 0-4-2T locomotive built at Wolverhampton in 1869 and bought by the Bishop's Castle Railway in 1905. (Lens of Sutton)

When in October 1865 the branch to Bishop's Castle was completed, it was decided to start services without waiting for either the Government Inspection of the line or the Montgomery extension. According to Edward Griffith in his booklet *The Bishop's Castle Railway 1865–1935*, passenger services commenced with a locomotive and eleven coaches probably borrowed from the Mid-Wales Railway for the occasion.

Bishop's Castle station had not yet been built but, despite this, large crowds turned out at noon to see the locomotive carrying inscriptions 'Better Late Than Never' and 'Long-Looked-For

Assorted items await collection at Bishop's Castle station. The branch opened in 1866 with four trains daily in each direction usually mixed freight/passenger. (Lens of Sutton)

Come at Last' hauling the coaches laden with shareholders and their friends. In the town, decorated with many arches of evergreen, a band played 'See the Conquering Hero Comes' as it headed a long procession. Later about 300 guests sat down to a banquet in a marquee erected on the bowling green adjoining the Castle Hotel. During the evening there was a firework display and the 'navvies' who had built the line were entertained with a meal of roast beef, plum pudding and ale.

Formal opening of the BCR came on 1st February 1866 when regular passenger services began. Initially there were four trains daily in each direction, mostly of a mixed freight/passenger nature. An early locomotive was 0-4-0ST named *Bee* which had been used during the construction of the line. This was disposed of after three years by which time 0-6-0 *Plowden* had taken its place. The fastest time for the journey was half an hour although many trains took up to 50 minutes for the 9¼ mile journey. Freight provided much of the traffic particularly on market days at Bishop's Castle and many wagons were borrowed from the GWR and LMSR to supplement the BCR's own meagre fleet.

Passenger traffic remained light throughout the life of the BCR. The station was fairly close to the town centre and no doubt the first regular passenger train of the day awoke many residents since it left for Craven Arms at 6.10 am. The last daily train returned from Craven Arms at 6.45 pm. In addition numerous excursions were run, usually associated with local football clubs or the annual Shrewsbury Floral Fete. In order to cater for such events, GWR rolling stock was frequently brought in.

Despite financial uncertainty, the BCR still reckoned to go ahead with the Montgomery and Minsterley lines. The company considered that the most expensive work had been done and that when completed many major routes would be available. However such hopes were dashed as 1866 progressed particularly when the Overend & Gurney Bank collapsed causing widespread financial panic throughout the country and affecting many small railways in

Where Bishop's Castle trains once left the main line, photographed here in July 1935 three months after closure. The branch failed through neglect and lack of passengers. (John H. Meredith)

Bishop's Castle station after closure. It was felt that had the line extended to Montgomery as originally planned, it might have proved more successful. (Lens of Sutton)

the course of construction. As a result, the BCR dropped its planned branches causing investment to slump. By the end of the year the BCR was close to bankruptcy and, when creditors could not be satisfied, the law was invoked.

Bailiffs were brought in with one at each terminus and a third accompanied the trains which continued to provide a service. A sale was organised at the George Hotel, Shrewsbury, and many of the company's assets were sold so that creditors could be paid. These included locomotives, goods and passenger vehicles which together realised £880. Eventually it was considered that the line could be made to pay and a Receiver was appointed to be responsible for the accounts.

All went fairly well for a number of years but ten years later, in February 1877, there was another crisis. Legal action was taken against the company by the widow of a director who had sold a parcel of land for £800 but had never been paid. The High Court agreed an order to pay and when this was not settled by the BCR, the railway was duly 'possessed' as from 27th February 1877. An extraordinary state of affairs was to follow.

The lawyers gave notice and, after proceeding to Horderley station, they removed a rail and built a fence across the track marking the boundary of the property in question. For a time a shuttle service continued between Bishop's Castle and Horderley from where passengers continued by horse-drawn coaches to Craven Arms. This however provided only a temporary solution and it was not long before Bishop's Castle ran very short of coal and other supplies. Desperate measures were needed and a 'council of war' was held in the back parlour of a well known Craven Arms inn.

According to an account in the *Railway Magazine*, a party fortified itself with the cellar's best whisky and later found itself in charge of a shunting engine conveniently heading a number of

*Eaton station in the
1930s. The building still
exists as a private
residence. On reaching
Lydham Heath trains had
to reverse for Bishop's
Castle. (Lens of Sutton)*

loaded trucks. Equally conveniently the signalman in charge of the junction, usually closed at night, was still in his cabin. Meantime two bailiffs guarding the removed section of track were lured to the Red Lion at Horderley where beer tempered with gin proved more comforting than keeping vigil outside on a cold dark night. No sooner had the bailiffs disappeared than a gang of men with lanterns restored the removed rail. The all-clear was given and an engine hauling empties quietly made its way down from Bishop's Castle to Craven Arms where it picked up the loaded trucks. With a good shove from the LNWR shunting engine, it then steamed as hard as it could for the beleaguered town.

When the bailiffs heard the train coming it was too late for action. They rushed from the Red Lion and waved their lanterns but to no avail. They had been outwitted and despite threats by the lawyers to carry out an arrest, the manager was able to prove an alibi. Although Bishop's Castle had been relieved, the event had not solved the BCR's problems and a meeting was held to discuss re-opening the railway.

Various options were discussed, ranging from selling privately, becoming part of the GWR or raising further cash. The last option was adopted even to the extent that a group of local people purchased a locomotive for £700 and then leased it back to the company. On Monday, 2nd July 1877, flags were hung in celebration once again in Bishop's Castle when the line re-opened. There were cheers when the first through train left for Craven Arms and, on its return, church bells were rung and shops were closed for the occasion.

Lydham Heath station was rebuilt around 1906 to consist of a wooden building with two waiting rooms and a small storage shed. It was here that an incident occurred which could have had more serious consequences. At Lydham Heath a reversal was necessary

Horderley station building today, tastefully converted to a private residence. A home signal and a short stretch of restored platform maintain the railway atmosphere. (Author)

and it was the usual custom for the locomotive to run round the train before going on to Bishop's Castle. Sometimes the train was pushed and there was an occasion when a 'helpful' individual uncoupled the engine on arrival thinking it would head the train. Unfortunately this was not so and it was not until the driver applied his brakes as he neared Bishop's Castle that he saw the coaches going on ahead! He whistled furiously to attract the guard's attention who fortunately stopped the coaches just in time.

Over the ensuing years the line struggled on and several attempts made to get the GWR to take over the line proved unsuccessful. By 1931 rumours of closure were rife. A Railway Users' Committee was formed to help the line but with road traffic successfully competing there was little it could do. Finally it was directed that on 20th April 1935 the line would close completely. Shortly before the end a train made a journey with just one passenger for the entire journey. During a stop at Eaton, the passenger noted with regret that the time-table posters had been torn from the walls of the waiting room. When this was pointed out to the station-master, back came the reply, 'No, not torn off. The goats have eaten them'.

Today the line is enthusiastically recalled by members of the Bishop's Castle Railway Society. A section of platform at Horderley has been restored, a signal has been erected and a station nameplate proudly added. Work has also progressed towards restoration of Glenburrel Bridge, the only complete bridge on the old trackbed. Finally a museum housing numerous fascinating relics of the BCR opened in Bishop's Castle during 1992, surely well worth a visit.

Chapter 6

SHROPSHIRE QUARRY LINES

(Ludlow/Bitterley Yard/Clee Hill Quarries and Bitterley Yard/
Titterstone Quarries, Cleobury Mortimer/Ditton Priors)

Ludlow/Bitterley Yard/Clee Hill Quarries and Bitterley Yard/
Titterstone Quarries
A visit to Titterstone Clee Hill can prove a sheer delight. From
the top, which stands at 1,750 feet above sea level, there are views
over many of the surrounding counties, an attractive spot indeed
for the walkers or sightseers who visit the area. Giant golfball-like
structures look down, described on the OS map as a Satellite Earth
Station. These objects control the paths of aircraft, a far cry indeed
from the cranking and groaning railway engines of yesteryear
which hauled their various mineral loads.

The Ludlow and Clee Hill Railway, incorporated on 22nd July
1861, was built solely to transport the vast quantities of mineral
from the summits of Titterstone Clee Hill and Clee Hill. The 4½
mile standard gauge section between Ludlow and Bitterley Yard
opened on 24th August 1864 but it was to be another three years
before a steep climb from Bitterley to the incline top at the small
village of Dhustone began working. The single-track line from
Ludlow to Bitterley included a gradient of 1 in 20, enough to strain
any locomotive, but with this next section climbing at 1 in 12 and
steepening to 1 in 6, it was necessary for loads to be worked by a
cable-operated funicular. The line, which rose 600 feet in 1¾
miles, included a passing loop, above which tracks converged with
a common middle rail to the summit. The system was operated by
a stationary steam engine in a winding drum house situated at the
top. The final section to Clee Hill Quarries was level by compari-
son, skirting the south side of the hill and connecting the incline

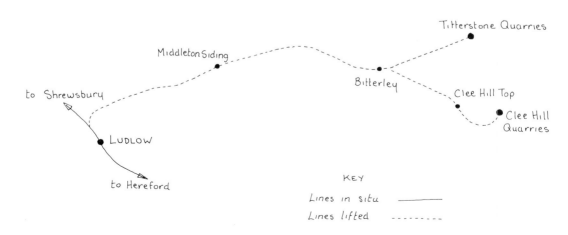

40

top with a quarry crushing plant. This required a shunting engine permanently based on the hillside section.

In addition to the Clee Hill Quarries line, another stretch of 1¾ miles climbed from Bitterley Yard to Titterstone Quarry on nearby Titterstone Clee Hill. This was a 3 feet gauge self-acting rail system, privately owned by British Quarrying Co Ltd, with the full trucks going down providing the momentum for those going up. This incline closed in 1952 but visiting the area today, it is possible to find where the incline crossed above the village of Bedlam (or Titterstone as it is now called). Abutments are still in existence just beyond Titterstone Cottages.

Minerals were lowered from the top of the Clee Hill Quarries standard gauge incline by four wagons plus a brake truck at a speed of not more than 6 mph. The maximum load permitted per wagon was 85 tons. On the Ludlow to Bitterley stretch there were problems when the rails were wet or slippery and it was not unusual for the tank locomotives coming from Ludlow to rush the gradient or even halve their loads. A water tower built at the foot of the gradient often proved necessary to drivers when the engines were struggling.

In 1893 the Ludlow & Clee Hill Railway was taken over by the Shrewsbury & Hereford (LNWR & GWR Joint). Business remained brisk and by the end of the First World War (1914–1918) the delivery of roadstone was even busier. There were times when around 6,000 tons of stone were being despatched from the quarries each week. By the 1930s, as roads improved, competition from lorries caused the rail traffic to fall away. Despite this, the branch remained active for some time yet. During its last years various LMS/GWR (later BR) locomotives worked the line. Four wheeled Sentinel engines (built 1928/1930) were a frequent sight as were two South Wales 0-4-0 saddle tanks, formerly with the Swansea Harbour Trust Railway as GWR 1142 and 1143. In fact

Ludlow station looking towards Hereford in earlier times. The station buildings today have gone, replaced by very basic structures. (Lens of Sutton)

41

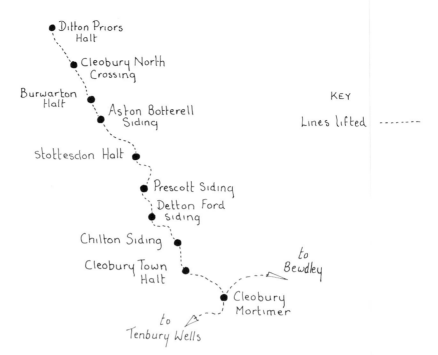

1143 was the last to work at Clee Hill prior to closure of the incline on 7th November 1960. Over two years later, on 31st December 1962, the line from Ludlow (Clee Hill junction) to Bitterley Yard closed officially.

Cleobury Mortimer/Ditton Priors

Parliament agreed the Cleobury Mortimer & Ditton Priors Light Railway (CM&DPLR) on 23rd March 1901, yet it took some seven years before the 12¾ mile line could open. There were financial problems and it was not until March 1906 that a tender was accepted. On 23rd January 1907 the first sod was cut although without any ceremony. Work commenced two days later and in June 1907 a connection was made with the GWR line at Cleobury Mortimer. The line opened to freight traffic on July 19th 1908 and a daily goods train initially hauled by contractor's locomotives was possible.

The CM&DPLR began its life with great hopes for the future. Much of the stone came from the Clee Hill Granite Company's Magpie Quarries on Titterstone Clee Hill from where it was carried by means of a 3½ mile aerial ropeway which reached the railway at Detton Ford Siding. Another quarry on Brown Clee Hill (1,771 ft) was operated by the Abdon Clee Stone Quarrying Company where stone was brought down a rope-worked incline to connect with a siding at Ditton Priors.

Passenger services on the CM&DPLR commenced on 21st November 1908 after a Board of Trade inspection of the line had been completed. At first, two mixed trains ran on certain weekdays only each way. Manning Wardle 0-6-0ST locomotives 1734

The remains of the trackbed at Clee Hill Top where trains were hauled by wire rope up a gradient steepening to 1 in 6 to the summit. (Author)

named *Burwarton* after Lord Boyne's estate and 1735 named *Cleobury* were available together with four four-wheeled oil-lit coaches. The latter were purchased from Bow Works in London, being conversions from North London Railway coaches.

Freight from the quarries brought considerable business with both the GWR and the Midland Railway bringing in their wagons. Occasionally passenger trains connected with Kidderminster where the market was popular and in August 1909 many travelled by rail to attend an Industrial, Horticultural and Poultry Show at Burwarton. On that occasion the line's capacity was stretched to its maximum when 300 extra passengers were catered for in one day. In 1910 some 15,000 passengers and 77,000 tons of freight were carried and in 1911 the operating surplus almost doubled.

In the couple of years leading up to the First World War passenger traffic fell disappointingly, a situation hardly surprising in such a rural area. Yet soon after hostilities had begun in 1914, freight traffic improved considerably. Stone from the quarries found new customers and quantities were railed regularly to

Cleobury Mortimer station served as a junction to the Cleobury Mortimer and Ditton Priors Light Railway. The station was situated about a mile and a half to the east of the town which meant that many passengers had to face a long and hilly walk. (Lens of Sutton)

Passengers' services on the Ditton Priors branch commenced on November 21st 1908 when two mixed trains ran on certain weekdays only. Picture taken at the Ditton Priors terminus soon after opening. (Lens of Sutton)

Aldershot. Wagons were soon in short supply and many more were acquired. The GWR lent class 850 0-6-0PT locomotive no 2001 to the CM&DPLR for a time to help out. As the war progressed freight traffic in timber also increased.

After the First World War the two locomotives, having now served over 10 years' faithful duty, took turns to go away to Worcester for repairs. In the same year 'peace' celebrations took place and to mark the event the Abdon Clee Quarry managing director treated his employees and all in the parish to a lavish tea. On 25th May 1922, following 'grouping', the CM&DPLR became part of the GWR.

The locomotives 1734 *Burwarton* and 1735 *Cleobury* therefore became GWR stock and they were renumbered nos 28 and 29. The GWR decided that they justified an extensive rebuild so they were both sent to Swindon. During their absence, 8650 class 0-6-0ST no 1948 and 0-6-0ST no 1970 were delivered from Kidderminster to keep the branch going. Both *Burwarton* and *Cleobury* were eventually returned to the branch rebuilt as pannier tank locomotives. Early in 1926 the four North London Railway

Burwarton station in earlier times. It was little used and it became a 'halt' in 1923. The station was in fact sited closer to Charlcotte than the village of Burwarton. (Lens of Sutton)

44

coaches were withdrawn and in their place came GWR gas lit four-wheeled coaches.

GWR 0-6-0PT no 29 waits with coaches in a siding at Cleobury Mortimer in 1935. The line played an important role during the 1939–1945 war when ammunition was stored in the area. (John H. Meredith)

By the early 1930s the quantities of stone carried had dropped considerably and traffic along the line was reduced to two mixed trains daily. Closure to passenger traffic became inevitable and local folk were hardly surprised when notices were displayed. Even so, petitions were organised to keep the line working but these had no effect. When the last passenger train ran on Saturday, 24th September 1938, so many people turned up that two extra four-wheeled carriages had to be added to the two already in use.

Yet as the passenger traffic ceased, so freight traffic received a dramatic boost. As a result of the 1938 Munich crisis, arms were being produced and the CM&DPLR area was considered safe for ammunition storage. Nissen huts were built along the line in readiness and, when hostilities began in September 1939, no 29 was sent to Worcester Works so that a spark arresting cowl could be fitted to her chimney. At first this was to protect ammunition vans from occasional sparks thrown out from the locomotive when tackling a gradient but later it was needed as a protection when working in the armament depot. The area was subsequently selected by the Admiralty as a Naval armament depot.

The one-time quiet branch was now a place of activity with the depot assuming strategic importance. The railway helped considerably with the war effort and since munition carriers were used, the speed limit was reduced to walking pace. Many were the occasions when crews had time to dismount and set snares by the trackside. The next day the same crews could be seen jumping down to collect their haul of rabbits!

In their book *The Cleobury Mortimer & Ditton Priors Light Railway*, W Smith and K Beddoes wrote that the depot even got a mention from the German wartime propagandist 'Lord Haw Haw'. Searchlights were installed at several places along the route and decoy fires were set up on the nearby Clee Hills. Happily the depot remained intact throughout the war.

In May 1957 the Admiralty took over complete ownership of the branch and five months later began operations with two Ruston and Hornsby 0-4-0 diesel shunters providing the occasional haulage power. Eventually traffic dwindled and on Good Friday, 16th April 1965, the line officially closed. Lifting of the track was delayed by removal of Admiralty equipment by rail from the depot. When track demolition began in earnest later in the year, suggestions were made that the line should be preserved but the difficulties appeared too great and the idea was dropped.

Numerous relics have survived to recall the earlier days. At the site of Cleobury Town station (on the B4363) the level crossing gate is still there at the side of the road. The coal yard still operates and, on entering, a length of rail (not in situ) can be seen to the left of the drive. The railway office built in 1917 has become a private residence and an old buffer stop helps form part of an end wall to a nearby garden shed.

To the north, the remains of Aston Botterell Siding can be found along a remote country lane. A small platform and a siding existed to serve the tiny hamlet nearby, yet traffic must have been almost negligible. All that is left is a weed-filled tumbledown shed where cattle sometimes take shelter and an indication where the track once passed.

Any vague hopes that the line might once again open were finally dashed in 1969 when army engineers were called in to blow up the bridge which crossed the Bewdley-Cleobury Mortimer road near the Blount Arms. According to local legend, a pot of gold sovereigns was bricked in when the bridge was built. Yet no trace was found. When the author visited the remains of the abutments in 1992 he had a poke around in the undergrowth – just in case.

Chapter 7

ALONG SHROPSHIRE'S BORDER

(Woofferton/Tenbury Wells/Bewdley)

Two miles from Newnham, close to the A456, the 1,250 yd long Southnet tunnel was built. The tunnel, a section of the Kington, Leominster and Stourport Canal, was completed in 1795 but it collapsed in the same year and, according to local rumours, two men and a boat are still entombed there! In all three large aqueducts, four tunnels (with one over two miles in length) and some 16 locks were planned, although in the event only a stretch of some 18 miles of continuous waterway, from Leominster to just beyond Newnham, was completed. The section, planned to open up a route to the river Severn as well as to the industrial Midlands, cost £93,000 to build but it did not prove successful and no dividend was ever paid to shareholders.

There was a proposal that the remainder of the journey to Stourport should be completed by tramway but this did not come about. What existed of the canal struggled through the first half of the 19th century to be eventually sold to the Shrewsbury & Hereford Railway (S&HR). The canal closed for good in 1859 although two years later stretches of it were to be used when a railway between Woofferton and Tenbury Wells was constructed.

The single track line between Woofferton, Tenbury Wells and Bewdley crossed the county boundaries of Worcestershire, Shrop-

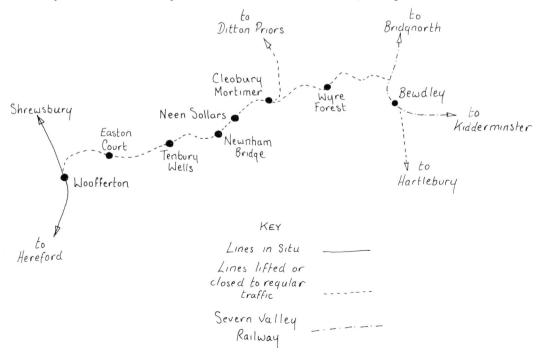

47

GWR Churchward class 4500 2-6-2T no 4596 waits at Woofferton station probably in the late 1940s. The station closed to passengers in July 1961. (Lens of Sutton)

shire and Herefordshire several times during its run through attractive and unspoilt countryside. The first section between Woofferton and Tenbury Wells, built by the Tenbury Railway with support from the S&HR, opened on August 1st 1861 and was worked by the GWR. Tenbury Wells remained a terminus for only three years after which time the Tenbury & Bewdley Railway, incorporated in 1860, completed the section to Bewdley. This was also GWR worked and it opened on 13th August 1864. Two companies now existed but the lines were soon integrated into one long section although a few trains did continue to run between Woofferton and Tenbury Wells only.

It seems there was at one time a difference of opinion as to how Woofferton should be spelled. During the 1930s the name Woofferton was spelled correctly on the nameboards, yet on the signal

Easton Court station on the line between Woofferton and Tenbury Wells seen here after closure. The station building is today a private residence.(Lens of Sutton)

box it read 'Wofferton' and on the platform trolleys it was spelt 'Wooferton'!

Leaving Woofferton station, the branch bore sharply eastwards along the Teme Valley where the first intermediate station was at Easton Court, known as 'Easton Court for Little Hereford'. The station closed to passengers only a year after opening but re-opened three years later in April 1865. Despite the sparsely populated locality, the station had a substantial building; today it is a private dwelling. At Little Hereford there was once an aqueduct which carried the Leominster Canal over the river Teme but, much to the annoyance of the local folk, this was blown up during the Second World War presumably to prevent its use by possible invaders!

In the 1840s Tenbury Wells had become established as a small spa, following the discovery of saline springs in the area. When trains reached the town in 1861 the station was situated in Burford, about half a mile from Tenbury Wells which lay to the south. Burford was the seat of Lord Northwick who, with a number of local landowners, had done much to get a railway into the area. Tenbury Wells had two platforms, a number of goods sidings and, in earlier years, a turntable. The station was initially known as just Tenbury but in 1912 it was renamed Tenbury Wells. After closure the station buildings were totally demolished and the site developed as an industrial estate although a road bridge still exists.

Enter a shop just up a short drive off the A456 at Newnham Bridge and you are in what was once the station building. Outside part of the station yard has become a garden centre. The platform and building remain intact but the station nameboard has been copied. To add further realism there is a signal and a truck at the end of the platform both of which were acquired from the Birm-

Tenbury Wells station which opened in 1861 as a terminus for a short branch from Woofferton. Today, completely demolished, the area is an industrial site. (Lens of Sutton)

49

ingham area. The single platform was sited so that access from the road had to be made over the track and strict instructions had to be issued to avoid the possibility of vehicles obstructing the running line. At times Newnham Bridge proved a busy station particularly when fruit was in season.

Beyond came Neen Sollars, a minor station which has survived as a private dwelling. Next was Cleobury Mortimer, sited about a mile and a half east of the town. Here the track layout was altered when the Cleobury Mortimer and Ditton Priors Light Railway opened in 1908 (see chapter 6). The remains of Cleobury Mortimer station can be found just to the south of the A4117 up a short drive by the Blount Arms. The station building is today private flats and, when visited by the author, the station nameboard still prominently displayed in the nearby undergrowth, 'Cleobury Mortimer. Change for Ditton Priors Railway'.

The last intermediate station before meeting the Severn Valley Railway at Bewdley was Wyre Forest where much of the track

The station nameboard which has survived amongst the weeds. Tracks to Bewdley and to Ditton Priors separated just to the north of the A4117 Cleobury Mortimer- Bewdley road.(Author)

wound its way through heavily graded curves. Today, difficult to find on a minor road, the station building and platform have survived as an attractive private residence. Outside by the roadway can be seen a discarded sleeper with a chair in situ and along the platform a concrete post which once supported fencing now has little more purpose than to carry a bird box.

Between Wyre Forest station and Bewdley the trackbed passes through the Wyre Forest Nature Reserve which is well worth a visit. Striking out from the visitor centre, found on the A456 two miles west of Bewdley, several designated walks can be taken where the forestry blends splendidly with the wildlife and where much of the area is also a Site of Special Scientific Interest. Walking a little further it is possible to find the trackbed alongside Dowles brook, not far from where the three span Dowles viaduct once carried trains over the river Severn.

In the early 1920s the branch saw five trains each way daily (none on Sundays) between Kidderminster and Woofferton and a further five made the daily 12 minute journey between Tenbury Wells and Woofferton. Various tank and tender locomotives were used on the line and when traffic was sparse it was not unusual to see an engine hauling a single carriage. In later years GWR diesel railcars were used for many of the passenger services.

After the war traffic suffered from road competition yet a proposal from British Rail in 1961 to close the line to passengers was strongly resisted. Despite this, the section from Woofferton to Tenbury Wells closed to all traffic on 31st July 1961 and Woofferton station was subsequently demolished. Regular passenger traffic between Tenbury Wells and Bewdley came to an end on 1st August 1962. After pressure BR did agree to provide an experimental passenger service between Tenbury and Bewdley comprising a weekday morning train and a return train in the evening but this lasted only a year ending on 1st August 1963. Goods services lasted a further year between Tenbury and Cleobury Mortimer terminating in January 1964 and the final stretch between Cleobury Mortimer and Bewdley (North junction) closed early in 1965.

Chapter 8

THE SEVERN VALLEY RAILWAY, A LINE RESTORED AND A CLIFF RAILWAY

(Shrewsbury/Bridgnorth/Bewdley/Hartlebury,
Bridgnorth/Bewdley/Kidderminster Town,
Bridgnorth's Castle Hill Railway)

Shrewsbury/Bridgnorth/Bewdley/Hartlebury

Had early railway planners had their way then the original Severn Valley Railway (SVR) would have consisted of double track providing a direct link between Shrewsbury and Worcester. In 1846 a survey was completed by Robert Nicholson who saw the line as a valuable link between numerous industrial and agricultural areas. The original estimate came to £600,000 but costs were considered too high and reductions in outlay were necessary. Savings of nearly a half of the original sum were effected by abandoning numerous bridges and by constructing single track. In addition it was decided to join the main Wolverhampton to Worcester trunk line at Hartlebury thus considerably shortening the distance.

Eventually in 1853 Parliament agreed such a line could be built but it was to be another nine years before it came into being. Regular services between Sutton Bridge junction, Shrewsbury and Hartlebury near Droitwich began on 1st February 1862 and they were worked initially by the West Midland Railway (WMR).

The formal opening took place on the previous day when a special train of twenty-two coaches left Worcester Shrub Hill bound for Shrewsbury. The passengers included the chairman of the GWR, the chairman of the SVR and the general manager of

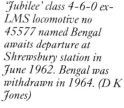

'Jubilee' class 4-6-0 ex-LMS locomotive no 45577 named Bengal awaits departure at Shrewsbury station in June 1962. Bengal was withdrawn in 1964. (D K Jones)

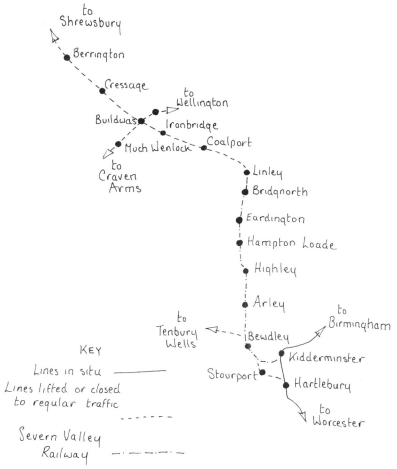

to
Shrewsbury

Berrington

Cressage

to
Wellington

Buildwas

Ironbridge

Much Wenlock

Coalport

to
Craven
Arms

Linley

Bridgnorth

Eardington

Hampton Loade

Highley

Arley

to
Tenbury
Wells

Bewdley

to
Birmingham

KEY

Kidderminster

Lines in situ ——————

Stourport

Lines lifted or closed
to regular traffic

Hartlebury

- - - - - - -

to
Worcester

Severn Valley
Railway   — · — · — · —

the WMR. At Shrewsbury three more coaches and an extra
locomotive were added after which the train returned non-stop to
Bridgnorth. Important guests ate from hampers and drank wine as
the train steamed slowly south, past the waving crowds on the
bridge at Iron Bridge and past the sightseers from Broseley who
had walked down into the Gorge to see the first train pass.
Commented *Shropshire Magazine*, 'Others aboard were less digni-
fied about refreshments, they ate pies and swilled them down with
beer'.

The line of almost 40 miles required fairly steep gradients
reaching 1 in 100 in places. Numerous viaducts were built and
tunnels included one of 594 yds at Bridgnorth to take the tracks
under the town and another between Bewdley and Stourport 480
yds long. Along the line there were 13 intermediate stations. Most
of these had two platforms and a loop, although a number began
their existence with just one platform and no loop.

The SVR provided four passenger trains each way daily with
further services available south of Bridgnorth. There were useful
amounts of freight, much of it agricultural and coal traffic coming
from the Highley area. Travelling southwards from Shrewsbury,

An Armstrong GWR 0-6-0 locomotive hauling a passenger train at Ironbridge & Broseley station c1910. The original Severn Valley Railway opened in 1862. (Lens of Sutton)

the first station was Berrington, although this was sited nearer to Cross Houses where a workhouse was converted to a Military Hospital during the First World War. Berrington station was kept busy during the war when trains brought wounded straight from the front.

After Cressage came Buildwas, where it was possible to catch trains to Much Wenlock and, from 1867, on to Craven Arms. Buildwas became a busy junction with its platforms at two levels and the station-master had a staff of ten. Two miles beyond, trains passed close to the well known Iron Bridge designed by Thomas Telford and erected in 1796.

At Coalport, the GWR and the LNWR rivalled each other for business with stations on opposite sides of the river. Next came Linley, which during its railway days boasted a very orderly station, often winning the prize for the best kept on the line. Bridgnorth followed, the station in later years to become part of the restored Severn Valley Railway.

After Eardington came Hampton Loade. Nearby it was possible to cross the river Severn by a barge running on an underwater cable which sometimes broke in heavy floods. There are many tales of boatmen and passengers being swept down the river as far as Arley. Highley station comprised a substantial building and a single platform. A loop allowed trains to pass and there were numerous sidings. In earlier days the nearby river Severn was busy indeed. The area boasted quarries of sandstone and shallow deposits of coal and it was from Highley that stone for Worcester Cathedral was carried downstream. The coal pits have gone but there are tales that at certain times of the year the ghosts of miners can still be seen walking through the village. After Arley came the principal station of Bewdley where trains continued via Stourport to Hartlebury.

On 18th July 1872 the SVR was absorbed into the GWR which in 1878 opened a link between Kidderminster and Bewdley. The latter became a crossing point with many Hartlebury trains running northwards to Bridgnorth and also Kidderminster trains which continued to run to Tenbury or Woofferton.

Throughout its life the SVR was never financially successful. The agricultural and coal traffic from the Highley area were among the SVR's principal sources of income. By the 1930s, despite increasing competition from the motor car, five trains were running daily from Hartlebury or Kidderminster to Shrewsbury with additional services covering the stretch to Bridgnorth. The number of passengers was diminishing so halts were opened in the hope of attracting further business. Many of the earlier tender locomotives had now gone and passenger trains were hauled by class 4500 2-6-2Ts. Diesel railcars were also making an appearance. Coal from Alveley Colliery, north of Highley, was generally hauled by class 4300 2-6-0s.

It was a sad day for many when the line closed between Shrewsbury and Bewdley. The last regular passenger train left Bridgnorth for Shrewsbury at 7.27 pm on Saturday, 7th September 1963, hauled by class 2 locomotive 2-6-2T no 41207. All that was left for passengers was a shuttle between Kidderminster, Bewdley, Stourport and Hartlebury. There were strong protests when closure of these lines was announced and a date planned for 7th April 1969 had to be postponed. Eventually when at 7.20 pm on Saturday, 3rd January 1970, the last train left Bewdley for Kidderminster, it seemed that passenger traffic along any part of the attractive Severn Valley had truly come to an end. Yet this was far from the case. Efforts to restore steam along the SVR had already been in hand for a number of years.

Bridgnorth/Bewdley/Kidderminster Town – A Line Restored
The Severn Valley Railway Society was formed on 6th July 1965 when a group of enthusiasts met at Kidderminster. North of Bridgnorth station track had been lifted but, between Alveley and Bewdley, BR still operated coal trains. The society set out to purchase the 6¾ mile disused section from Bridgnorth to Alveley

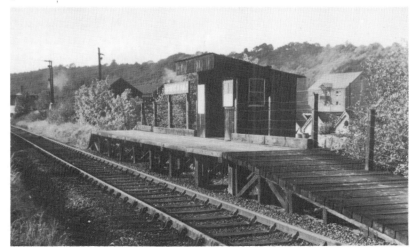

Jackfield Halt, between Ironbridge and Coalport, which opened in March 1954 to replace an earlier halt opened in 1934 but which was destroyed in 1952 in a landslip. (Lens of Sutton)

which had fortunately not yet been lifted. The intention was to run passenger trains from Bewdley to Hampton Loade (4¼ miles) and after two weeks of negotiation a price of £25,000 was agreed with BR to cover all freehold land, buildings and track. A deposit of 10% was paid the following year and within a further three years, after considerable fund raising, the remainder was paid.

There was great excitement when, on Saturday, 23rd May 1970, the first public passenger train left Bridgnorth. Six GWR coaches were hauled by 2251 class ex-GWR locomotive no 3205 to Hampton Loade and back with an hourly service following. Meantime in 1969 Alveley Colliery had closed and SVR members' eyes were already looking further southwards. With Bewdley closed by BR to passengers in January 1970, the way seemed clear to press through Bewdley to Foley Park, near Kidderminster. A further campaign followed, ably assisted by the late Sir Gerald Nabarro, MP for Worcester South since 1961, who was also a rail enthusiast. The target of £110,000 was reached and £74,000 was spent on purchasing the railway to Foley Park.

After a tremendous effort by Severn Valley engineering volunteers, Highley was reached in April 1974 with Bewdley following one month later. The final goal of reaching Kidderminster seemed within the SVR's reach but further obstacles had to be overcome. The two-mile section from Bewdley to Foley Park, although purchased by the SVR in 1974, had been used only on special occasions such as steam trains at Enthusiast Weekends. Sugar factory traffic between Foley Park and Kidderminster ceased in 1980 but the line remained available to link BR with the SVR. Kidderminster remained a firm target but problems persisted. BR traffic between Stourport junction and Worcester had become so poor that closure of the section was considered. Happily for the SVR the line was saved when local services between Gloucester and Birmingham were routed via Kidderminster instead of Bromsgrove, the latter stretch being needed for new High Speed Trains from May 1983.

During 1983/4 over £370,000 was raised by share issue and out of this £75,000 was used to purchase the stretch of line between

Eardington Halt in earlier Severn Valley Railway days when it served as a useful stopping place with watering facilities.(Lens of Sutton)

Foley Park and Kidderminster junction. The balance was to be used to develop the former BR goods-yard site at Comberton Hill to form a new SVR 'Kidderminster Town' station. Finally on 30th July 1984 the great day came. The first train to enter Kidderminster was a VIP special headed by 4-6-0 no 4930 *Hagley Hall*.

Today the Severn Valley Railway continues in popularity bringing pleasure to the many thousands of visitors who travel the line throughout most of the year. With its many enthusiastic and voluntary supporters, it is worth recalling that the Severn Valley Railway has the largest collection of locomotives and rolling stock in the UK.

Highley station with its single platform and loop photographed in 1989. Earlier a footbridge had crossed the line but after closure of Highley in 1963 it deteriorated and was demolished. (Author)

A stiff penalty for not shutting the gate at the end of Highley station platform! (Author)

A view down the 1 in 1.5 slope at Bridgnorth's cliff railway. The rise of 111 ft claims to be the steepest gradient in the country. (Author)

A Cliff Railway at Bridgnorth

Whilst visiting the Severn Valley Railway at Bridgnorth it is also worth paying a visit to the town's Castle Hill Railway (known as The Lift) which provides a useful link between Underhill Street in the Low Town and Castle Terrace in the High Town area. Built in 1891/1892, it was necessary to cut 50 ft into the sandstone in order to preserve the scenery in the area. During the excavations, caves were discovered at the lower end and one was so large that masonry columns and girders had to be erected. The railway opened on July 7th 1892.

The cars on the 3 ft 8 in gauge double-track were initially operated on the water balance principle. Each housed a 2,000 gallon water tank and the upper car was filled with water from a tank on the station roof until it was sufficiently heavy to pull up the car at the lower end. The water used was pumped back to the top by independent gas engines.

In April 1933 it was decided to close the railway but it re-opened just over a year later after control had been acquired by new shareholders. In December 1944 an electrically-driven drum haulage system was installed at the top. New carriages were fitted to the existing chassis in 1955 being of a modern tramcar design and each capable of seating 18 passengers.

The line, used throughout the year, is 201 ft long and with a vertical rise of 111 ft. When the Lynton & Lynmouth Cliff Railway opened in April 1890 it claimed to be the steepest railway in the country with a gradient of 1 in 1.8 but when Bridgnorth's Castle Hill Railway opened just over two years later, it gained the honour with a gradient of 1 in 1.5.

When visited in July 1992 business was brisk despite poor weather. It was perhaps cosier in the control office at the top where Chalkie the cat curled comfortably under a shelf. On receipt of a signal from below the cars set off. The fare was 28p – a small price to pay to avoid over 200 steps!

Chapter 9

A LINE TO STAFFORD AND RIVALS ACROSS THE SEVERN

(Wellington/Newport/Stafford, Wellington/Oakengates/Coalport (East))

Wellington/Newport/Stafford

There was a day in 1852 which villagers of Donnington, just to the north of Telford, would have long remembered. The trouble began at Shrewsbury when on 29th July a train from Stafford arrived with the driver complaining that the LNWR locomotive *Mazeppa* no 24, a 2-2-2 of Trevithic-Allan design built at Crewe in 1849, had problems. The foreman instructed the night cleaner, Thompson, to deal with it but early next morning when the driver arrived to prepare the engine he found it was missing. Thompson had earlier 'fired' *Mazeppa* but had left the engine in forward gear with the regulator open.

It was soon realised that the locomotive with no-one aboard was steaming towards Stafford. There was an immediate hue and cry and another available engine was sent in hot pursuit. The driver soon saw flying steam in the distance but he could do nothing. It was not until Donnington that the runaway engine came to an unfortunate stop, crashing into the back of an early train bound for Stafford and killing one of the few passengers. Thompson was woken from his sleep at Shrewsbury to find himself facing a charge of manslaughter.

The line from Wellington to Stafford began its life by an Act of Parliament dated 3rd August 1846 submitted by the Shropshire Union Railways & Canal Company (SUR&CC). The company was soon to become a pawn in the battles between the LNWR and

Earlier days at Wellington Salop, today known as Wellington Telford West, when trains ran direct to Stafford, a branch which closed to passengers in 1964. (Lens of Sutton)

the GWR to reach the Mersey. Less than a year later the SUR&CC was leased to the LNWR.

Earlier there had been numerous ambitious plans put forward by the SUR&CC, many of these comprising lines to be built along the banks of bankrupted canals. Such routes included a branch from Stafford to Stone in the Potteries plus another between Crewe and Newtown in Wales. Canal owners had been forced to gradually give way to railway schemes as the railways proved themselves superior and the canal company's plans to convert further long stretches of canals never materialised.

The Wellington to Stafford line opened on 1st June 1849, the same day that services commenced between Shrewsbury and Oakengates. Most people welcomed the trains which provided new links with the rest of the country and it was expected that the agricultural and industrial trades would greatly benefit. The line from Stafford junction to Wellington was 18¼ miles in length and for a time it had the advantage that it was the only link between Shrewsbury and London. By taking a train to Stafford, passengers could continue on the LNWR to Euston. Three trains daily connected with London trains and this was doubled within a year or so. However fares were not cheap for the second class cost to travel from Shrewsbury to Stafford was 3s 10d (19p) and the fare to London (also 2nd class) was £1, a figure well above the average weekly wage. 3rd class or 'Parliamentary' trains were available but these generally left Shrewsbury between 3 am and 5 am in the morning which to most was quite unacceptable.

In the 1950s scores of steam trains stopped at Wellington daily. Here ex-LMS 2-6-2T no 41232 hauls the 1.02 pm from Crewe on 12th August 1963. (D K Jones)

Meantime the Shrewsbury & Birmingham Railway (S&BR) was struggling to reach Birmingham. Wet weather held up work on large embankments at Shifnal and also work in Oakengates tunnel. There was further aggravation when Sunday working was introduced, with clerics complaining it was a 'flagrant violation of the

Gnosall station on the Wellington to Stafford branch closed completely in September 1964. Parts of the former Down platform booking office can be found today at the Foxfield Railway at Caverswall Road station. (Courtesy Staffordshire County Museum, Shugborough)

Sabbath'. It was to be another five years before Birmingham was reached but, when completed, it meant that passengers could travel 30 miles directly from Shrewsbury to Birmingham instead of 46 miles via Stafford. A bitter price war began and after massive reductions by the SUR&CC, the price dropped to as little as one penny (less than ½p) for ten miles. People were quick to take advantage and trains into Shrewsbury from around Newport and Wellington were often carrying over a thousand passengers each!

The Wellington/Stafford line left the S&BR line at Stafford junction with its first intermediate station at Hadley. As a village Hadley dates back to Saxon times and has numerous claims to fame. Hadley Park Mill, powered by both water and steam, was probably the only such mill of its kind in Shropshire and a lock at Hadley Park was last used in the 1930s. During the 18th century Hadley Park Hall was occupied by the celebrated ironmaster, John Wilkinson, who was well regarded by the local folk. So well, in fact, that many thought his ghost would return on the 7th anniversary of his death to pull the old industries out of a recession. Thousands gathered and waited (and still wait?) but he did not return.

After Trench Crossing and Donnington, the next station was Newport. Although a village, this was the only intermediate station of any significance for in later years few passengers used the service beyond to Stafford. Today much of the former trackbed has gone and the station has been completely demolished to make

Ex-LMS 2-6-2T class 3P no 40058 in steam at Coalport in early BR day. The station name changed to Coalport East to avoid confusion with the GWR Coalport station across th river Severn. (Lens of Sutton)

way for a housing estate. Passing through Newport on the A41 it is possible to see a redundant road bridge to the east across a field. There is yet another reminder of Newport at the Blists Hill Museum at Iron Bridge. The station crane was removed there in 1973.

At Gnosall the embankments can be determined each side of the A483 on entering the village. The Shropshire Union Canal passes through Gnosall linking Market Drayton and beyond to the north and Wolverhampton to the south. Gnosall's railway bridge across the A483 has gone but when in existence it carried the initials SUR (Shropshire Union Railways). Happily the station's down booking office has been saved, residing today in the main entrance to the Foxfield Railway at Caverswall Road station at Blythe Bridge in North Staffordshire (chapter 14). The last station before Stafford was Haughton. Although the area has considerably increased in population over the last few decades, it still retains much of its rural character. The manor house with its close-timbered black and white building dates back to the 16th century and the barn, now a cottage, boasts timbers reclaimed from sailing ships.

The Wellington/Stafford branch, like so many, fell victim to road competition and closed to passengers on 7th September 1964. Freight lingered awhile but this too closed between Newport and Stafford on 1st August 1966. Further stretches followed leaving only the Wellington/Donnington section open. This was singled in July 1971 and track still exists today.

Wellington/Oakengates/Coalport (East)
The main aim of the LNWR branch from Wellington to Coalport

was to break the GWR dominance of traffic in the industrial area to the south. The GWR had access to the ironworks and pits whereas the LNWR had to make do with the Shropshire Canal, an independent branch of the Shropshire Union Canal which ran from Trench to Coalport. The canal however was suffering badly from shortage of water and subsidence and it was estimated that some £30,000 was needed for repairs. Rather than face this, the LNWR agreed in 1856 to build a single track branch from Wellington (Hadley junction) to Coalport.

The LNWR obtained powers to buy and convert part of the canal by an Act agreed on 27th July 1857. The line was built along the canal to a point east of Dawley and then winding southwards to Brookside and Tweedale and on to Coalport adjacent to the river Severn. On the opposite bank of the river some eight months later was to come the GWR Coalport station and this no doubt caused confusion for passengers although this was clarified in later days when the LNWR station was renamed Coalport East. There were frequent plans to build a bridge across the river at Coalport but they never transpired.

The single-track branch opened on 17th June 1861 although passenger traffic was never heavy. Trains took over half an hour to reach Coalport from Wellington and the original third class fare was 8d (3½p) for the whole journey. The trains gained the nickname of the 'Coalport Dodgers'. The line's existence was mostly justified by its freight traffic.

The branch became an early victim of road competition with passenger traffic ending on 2nd June 1952. Goods traffic kept the branch alive for a further 12 years, a time when 'Cauliflower' 0-6-0s and Webb coal tanks were much in evidence. After complete closure a section of the branch was used for a time by the Telford Horsehay Steam Trust when a 2 ft gauge Telford Town tram ran alongside Randlay Lake in Town Park. But it rarely got the opportunity to work publicly and, despite plans to extend, for various reasons it had to close. What a missed opportunity!

A steam passenger train awaits departure at Coalport East station. Traffic was never heavy on the branch from Wellington and trains gained the nickname 'The Coalport Dodgers'. (Lens of Sutton)

Young admirers watch as LMS 4-6-0 class 6P locomotive no 46114 Coldstream Guardsman awaits departure at Stafford station on 12th July 1962. (D K Jones)

Four miles of the former trackbed are today part of the 14 mile long Silkin Way, a walkway named in honour of Lord Silkin who pioneered Telford New Town. To the south the Silkin Way leads to the Blists Hill Open Air Museum which is part of the Ironbridge Gorge Museum. Here it is possible to see restored plateway trucks, some of these reputed to have been in use as late as the 1950s.

Chapter 10

GWR LINES AT MUCH WENLOCK
AND A BRANCH TO SHIFNAL

(Wellington/Lightmoor/Buildwas/Much Wenlock/Craven Arms,
Wellington/Lightmoor/Madeley/Shifnal)

As early as the 16th century coal was exported from mines at
Madeley and Broseley via the river Severn and two centuries later
traffic had reached 100,000 tons per year. In 1709 came successful
experiments when Abraham Darby (1677–1717) began to use
coke made from local coal and not charcoal as a fuel to smelt iron.
Cast-iron plate rails were constructed in 1767, representing a
transitional stage between the thin wrought-iron plates previously
in use and the edge rail which superseded them.

The ironworks and collieries in the district continued to flourish
through the 19th century and, to improve transportation, the
Shrewsbury & Birmingham Railway (S&BR) planned to bring a
branch line into the area. On 1st June 1854 a four-mile freight
line from Shifnal (the S&BR's only branch) opened via Madeley
to Coalbrookdale. Three months later, in September 1854, the
S&BR became part of the GWR.

Meantime on 28th August 1853, the Wellington & Severn
Junction Railway (W&SJR) was authorised to build a line from
Wellington to Lightmoor. The 'turning of the first sod' in August
1855 proved quite an event. A newspaper reported 'a series of
festivities of the most joyous nature'. At an early hour on the great
day, the people of Wellington woke to the firing of a cannon from
the Shropshire Works. Later folk were able to tour the vast works
that constructed all the articles connected with the railway from
'the simple wood blocks to hold rails on the sleeper to the carriages
which roll over them'.

At one o'clock there was a grand procession which included

*Horsehay & Dawley
station, c1910, on the
branch from Wellington to
Buildwas which closed to
passengers in 1962. Close
to the station site today is
the Telford Horsehay
Steam Trust where many
fascinating exhibits can be
seen.(Lens of Sutton)*

twelve navvies in white smocks carrying picks and shovels, a banner stating 'All Friends around the Wrekin' and another reading 'Success to the Wellington & Severn Junction Railway'. The ceremony was carried out in a field adjoining the S&BR where Mr Williams, representing the contractor, dug up several sods, put them in a wheelbarrow, wheeled them along a plank and tipped them out at the end. There was much cheering, the National Anthem was played and champagne corks popped.

The W&SJR opened to freight between Ketley junction (on the S&BR line) and Horsehay Ironworks on 15th May 1857 with passenger services following on 2nd May 1859. These were extended to Lightmoor on 1st August 1861 where trains reversed, providing a through service via Madeley on to Shifnal back on the main S&BR line. Horsehay (known as Horsehay & Dawley) was the largest intermediate station. It had a busy yard with ten sidings including two which served the Horsehay Ironworks.

On 1st February 1862 the Severn Valley Railway opened (chapter 8) providing four trains daily in each direction from Shrewsbury to join the main Birmingham to Worcester line at Hartlebury. On the same day the Much Wenlock & Severn Junction Railway connected with services between Buildwas and Much Wenlock. All that remained to allow through services from Much Wenlock to Wellington was a rail connection across the river Severn through to Lightmoor and this followed on 1st November 1864. The bridge across the river Severn, known as the Albert Edward Bridge, was constructed by the Coalbrookdale Company.

The final stretch of 14 miles to complete a through line from Wellington to Craven Arms was completed by the Wenlock Railway (or to give it its full title – The Much Wenlock, Craven Arms and Coalbrookdale Company). From Much Wenlock the single track line met the Shrewsbury & Hereford Railway (S&HR) at Marsh Farm junction, north of Craven Arms. The line had been agreed by an Act of 1861 but it took over six years to complete, mainly because of local opposition from landowners at Presthope.

Buildwas Junction where trains ran southwards to Much Wenlock or northwards to Wellington. Here passengers could change for the original Severn Valley line. Behind the station, the now demolished Buildwas A Power Station. (Lens of Sutton)

This caused the railway to move from its originally planned course south of Wenlock Edge to tunnel through the Edge west of Presthope at considerably extra cost.

The line opened on 5th December 1864 as far as Presthope where a temporary terminus was built. The remainder to Marsh Farm junction was completed on 16th December 1867 when at last trains could reach Craven Arms. Considerable improvements were made at Much Wenlock station with the original station building becoming a goods shed. The sidings were numerous and the small signal box had a potential of as many as 31 levers.

The entire branch was regarded as one of the most scenic in the British Isles with the journey giving fine views along the steeply graded sections. After leaving the main Wolverhampton line, trains climbed westward on a 1 in 50 gradient to reach Ketley, a single platform with substantial buildings. Ketley Town Halt and New Dale Halt (which opened in the 1930s to encourage traffic) were followed by Lawley Bank. The gradient now dropped sharply to 1 in 40 to reach Horsehay & Dawley, a rather gloomy station area improved only by the early summer display of rhododendrons along the opposite bank. Beyond Doseley Halt came Lightmoor junction where the Madeley branch trailed in from the left. This was followed by Lightmoor Halt which opened in 1907, then known as Lightmoor Platform and of wooden and corrugated-iron construction.

Descending towards the river, trains passed Green Bank Halt and Coalbrookdale, where the famous iron works could be seen in the valley to the left. Coalbrookdale became a fully staffed station with a tiled platform and substantial brick buildings giving evidence to its importance. At Buildwas it was possible to see the

The line between Much Wenlock and Craven Arms closed to passengers in 1951 but the section northwards to Wellington lasted a further 11 years. Much Wenlock station building exists today as private properties. (Lens of Sutton)

(now demolished) Buildwas A Power Station. Beyond the river Severn the scenery became even more picturesque as trains made a steep and twisting ascent cutting through the limestone in Farley Dingle to reach Wenlock Edge, a line of unbroken hill from Iron Bridge to the Church Stretton Gap. Farley Halt opened in 1934 comprising a wooden shelter and platform, the area becoming busy during the Second World War when a siding led to a large underground petrol store.

Much Wenlock followed, a town of considerable historic importance with its attractive old houses and inns. As might be expected, the station building was constructed of imposing Gothic stone and there was a large and picturesque rockery on the opposite side of the single line. The station building remains very much in existence today having been converted to private residences.

After climbing to Corve Dale, trains reached Westwood Halt (opened 1935) to then descend to the foot of Wenlock Edge at Presthope, the temporary terminus from 1864 to 1867. The line then passed through a tunnel (207 yds) to reappear at Easthope Halt (opened 1936). Longville and Rushbury both had sturdy red-brick buildings and the latter had a fine garden with ornamental fir trees. Longville station survives today as a somewhat derelict building and overgrown platform but remarkably the station name-board is still in existence. The station building at Rushbury also lives on, as a private residence. Rushbury nestles under Wenlock Edge, in the valley of Apedale, sometimes referred to as 'The Valley of the Bees'. This is because of the bee-keeping done in the area by the monks of Wenlock Abbey during the 13th century. The last station on the branch was Harton Road after which the

Longville station building and platform, although somewhat derelict, were still there when visited in July 1992, some 30 years since a train last called. (Author)

single track joined the Shrewsbury to Hereford main line.

Around the turn of the century Wolverhampton-built 0-6-0 saddle tanks provided the motive power but from May 1906 steam railmotor units were used. These ran into difficulties on the various gradients and were replaced a year later by 2-4-0 tanks, although in later years class 44XX 2-6-2 tanks dominated the line. In 1937 diesel railcars were tried but these also were defeated by the gradients. As road competition increased so passenger receipts dropped, particularly on the Much Wenlock to Craven Arms section. Often the pick-up freight between Longville and Craven Arms consisted of one solitary engine and brake van.

Sections of the the Much Wenlock line were closed to passengers over a number of years from 31st December 1951. The first to go was the Much Wenlock to Craven Arms stretch with the line between Longville and Marsh Farm junction closing to freight as well. A strange situation then arose for although services from Much Wenlock to Longville closed officially, passengers could continue to travel on to Longville for some two years afterwards. This came about because a parcels service remained in existence by extending the working of a passenger train from Wellington and, guard willing, it was possible to travel on to Longville. Stranger still perhaps, British Rail even marked the Much Wenlock – Longville section as open to passengers on some of its system maps!

It is sad to reflect that when the Wellington – Buildwas – Much Wenlock section closed on 23rd July 1962, Much Wenlock station saw its busiest day. Over 200 people thronged the platform when the last passenger train left for Wellington at 7.05 pm. It was packed to capacity and was hauled by 2-6-2 tank locomotive no

69

Ex-LMS 4-6-0 no 45655 at Craven Arms around 1950 on the Hereford to Shrewsbury line, also the southern end of the Much Wenlock branch. The station was once an important junction where one could change for places such as Bishop's Castle, Wellington or Market Drayton. (Lens of Sutton)

4178 which carried a board reading 'The Beeching Special'.

The spirit of the earlier days of railways lives on today close to the site of the former Horsehay & Dawley station where the Telford Horsehay Steam Trust (Telford HST) has many exhibits. These include many unique standard and narrow gauge locomotives and items of rolling stock. One fascinating display is the only steam tram, 2ft gauge, in Britain, first sited at Telford Town Park and moved to its present location in 1988. This was a four-wheeled 16-seater vehicle with open 3rd class accommodation.

The Telford HST has made great progress since it was established in 1976 with the assistance of the Telford Development Corporation. In May 1984 track was re-opened between Horsehay Yard and Heath Hill Tunnel and in December 1985 the line to Horsehay & Dawley station was re-opened. The eventual aim of the Trust is to relay the former GWR section from Horsehay & Dawley to Lightmoor junction and ultimately to link across the Iron Bridge by-pass to British Rail at the site of the former Lightmoor station. Telford Steam Railway is operated entirely by volunteers and any offers of help by becoming members of the Steam Trust will always be welcomed.

Chapter 11

ACROSS COUNTY BORDERS

(Wellington/Market Drayton/Nantwich)

Wellington was once a town which boasted an important railway junction where many lines met. Apart from being on the main Shrewsbury to Birmingham route, branches carried trains on LNWR (later LMS) lines to Coalport and to Stafford while GWR branches led southwards to Much Wenlock and northwards to Market Drayton and on to Nantwich in Cheshire. This last route, now closed, wound its way across county borders and has been called a forgotten line, for today very little remains and nowhere along its route has any attempt been made to preserve any section.

Wellington (Salop) station, as it was known earlier, dates back to a time in 1849 when the Shrewsbury & Birmingham Railway was pressing eastwards to Birmingham. Originally Wellington possessed a single platform, since which time an island platform has been built on the 'up' side and bays have been added to accommodate the Coalport and Much Wenlock trains. In the early 1900s Wellington station was a very different place to the present Wellington Telford West station. There was much activity with upwards of 180 arrivals or departures of passenger trains each weekday. The first train of the day was the 1.30 am 'Isle of Man Boat Express' from Paddington which called at Wellington at 5.07 am. Other important trains included 'The Cambrian Express' and daily South Coast trains. One came from Birkenhead travelling to Ramsgate, Dover and Deal and another from Manchester via Crewe to reach Portsmouth. Expresses between Paddington and Birkenhead were frequent callers, often hauled by King or Castle locomotives covering the journey between Wellington and Paddington in about three hours.

Subsequently Wellington has seen many changes. Its engine

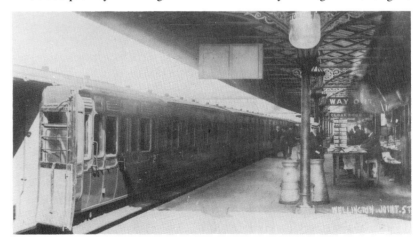

Wellington in 'GWR/ LNWR Joint' days c1910 when the station served as an important junction. Today the branch lines have gone and the station is called Wellington Telford West. (Lens of Sutton)

Crudgington on the Wellington/Market Drayton branch. In this 1910 picture, station staff seem to outnumber the passengers, although freight from a nearby creamery later proved profitable. (Lens of Sutton)

shed which housed mainly large Prairie tanks and panniers closed in 1964 and, with the closure of the Coalport and Much Wenlock branches, numerous signal boxes were demolished. Its parcels office, once regularly crammed with bicycles, prams and the like, has gone and the busy W H Smith bookstall is a thing of the past. The through daily South Coast expresses, often with Southern Railway green coaches, have long since been forgotten.

On 7th June 1861 Parliament approved the Nantwich & Market Drayton Railway. A year later on 7th August 1862 the Wellington & Drayton Railway was incorporated. Both companies were GWR supported which considered the connections to be of considerable importance giving it access to both Crewe and Stoke-on-Trent. There had previously been a number of unsuccessful schemes in the area including the Sheffield, Shrewsbury & South Wales Direct Railway which planned a route via Leek, Whitmore (crossing the main Crewe/Stafford line), Market Drayton and Hodnet. The GWR was anxious to thwart plans submitted; also it opposed a proposal submitted by the Wellington & Cheshire Junction Railway for a line from Wellington to Market Drayton, Nantwich and Northwich.

The 11 mile long branch from Nantwich to Market Drayton came first, opening on 20th October 1863 and four years later, on 16th October 1867, the Market Drayton to Wellington section of just over 16 miles was completed. The through route was classed as a secondary main line, stations were far apart and passengers were few. Three years later the North Staffordshire Railway (NSR) reached Market Drayton from Stoke, a line which served the industrial areas west of Stoke-on-Trent.

Travelling northwards from Wellington, trains branched away from the main Shrewsbury line, past Admaston to Bratton. The latter is the most northerly point of the 14 mile long Silkin Way walkway which crosses Telford New Town from the river Severn. The first intermediate station was Crudgington close to where the

rivers Strine and Tern meet. In the early 1920s a farmers' co-operative was set up at Crudgington which sent milk to London in the winter and made cheese in the summer. It became a true Creamery, collecting only cream for butter making and was taken over by the Milk Marketing Board in 1935. Today the complex of buildings houses a Research and Development Establishment as well as being a depot with packaging units trading under the well known logo 'Dairy Crest'. Beyond Crudgington came Peplow station, serving a truly rural area of scattered farms which could hardly have attracted many passengers.

The next station, Hodnet, had its busiest days on Tuesdays when both GWR and NSR trains arrived with passengers going to market. The NSR trains came via Market Drayton having been extended over GWR tracks to avoid a two hour wait at Market Drayton for a connection. At Tern Hill trains crossed the river

Market Drayton station not long before closure. NSR services to Stoke closed in 1956 but GWR trains between Wellington and Nantwich lasted until 1963. (Lens of Sutton)

Tern by a low three-arched bridge. The station was sited where the A53 crosses the A41, an overbridge on the latter having been demolished since closure to allow a road improvement. Passengers were few although there was additional traffic in the early 1920s when a large aerodrome was established nearby.

Market Drayton derived the first part of its name from the markets that have been held there for over 750 years. Each Wednesday it is possible to join in a bustling, bargain hunting tradition in traffic-free streets and under the old Buttercross. One of the town's celebrated products is gingerbread, faithful to recipes up to 200 years old and made by the local bakers' shops.

There were only two intermediate stations between Market Drayton and Nantwich, these being Adderley and Audlem. Adderley station served nearby Adderley Hall and it was near Audlem that the railway criss-crossed the Shropshire – Cheshire border. Audlem is perhaps better known today for its canal and series of locks. It is recorded that Moss Hall (near Audlem station) had three subterranean passages entered through secret doors. These were reputed to be places used by the family living at the Hall to hide from Cromwell's army. Nantwich's first railway came in 1858 when the Shrewsbury & Crewe Railway completed its line, five years before GWR trains entered the town.

In the early 1920s there were six stopping trains each way on weekdays between Wellington and Nantwich and only one on Sunday. In an effort to increase passenger traffic in the early 1930s, the GWR opened seven halts but it did little to help. The line became considerably busier during electrification of the main line from London through Crewe and for a time its prospects looked good. But this did not last and the familiar downward trend followed. Passenger services survived until 9th September 1963,

the same day the original Severn Valley Railway trains via Bridg-north were withdrawn. Freight services lasted only another four years.

A final indignity came to the branch when it was suggested that the Market Drayton to Nantwich stretch might become a walkway. Whereas the short section from Wellington to Bratton became part of the Silkin Way, local authorities in Cheshire were less co-operative considering the trackbed to be unsuitable.

Audlem on the Market Drayton to Nantwich branch, an area better known today for its canal and locks. When traffic dwindled in the early 1930s, the GWR opened halts but it made little difference. (Lens of Sutton)

Chapter 12

NORTH STAFFORDSHIRE LINES FROM STOKE-ON-TRENT

(Stoke/Silverdale/Market Drayton, Keele/Audley/Alsager Road/ Harecastle, Harecastle/Sandbach)

Stoke/Silverdale/Market Drayton

Earlier this century the village of Norton-in-Hales, close to the Shropshire/Staffordshire border, boasted three public houses and shops which included a butcher's, a general stores and a laundry. Not far away, where the lane climbed over the single-track railway line, could be found Norton-in-Hales station. Special trains used to run from Stoke bringing large crowds to the village for the annual harvest festivals and afterwards the Market Drayton Town Band played whilst a meal was provided under canvas in the rectory grounds.

When visited in May 1992, there was only one pub and a general stores/post office and the railway had long since gone. The station building plus part of the awning was still there, rescued from dereliction by Dennis Parton and his wife. But the railway spirit lives on for Dennis Parton has spent many years working for British Rail and living in the nearby former station-master's house, his father-in-law, Jack Woodcock, has also spent time on the railway. He worked first for the GWR and then the LMS, with much of his time of over 30 years as a signalman at Madeley.

The North Staffordshire Railway (NSR) opened a freight line from Stoke to Silverdale in 1852. It was initially intended to go no further, content to serve the various nearby collieries. Following a proposal from the Shrewsbury & Potteries Junction Railway (later to merge to become the famous 'Potts' railway) to build a line from Wellington via Madeley to Crewe, plus a branch to Silverdale, the London & North Western Railway (LNWR) supported the move but the proposal was, as expected, strongly opposed by the NSR. The plan never materialised and when the Great Western Railway (GWR) planned a line in 1862 from North Shropshire via Market Drayton to Manchester, the LNWR and NSR joined forces and blocked the idea. The GWR, not giving up easily, revived the plan but it was rejected by the House of Lords. As a result, the NSR felt it necessary to build westwards to Market Drayton to thwart any further GWR attempts.

To achieve such a plan, it was first necessary for the existing privately-owned Silverdale & Newcastle Railway (built in 1850 by iron master Ralph Sneyd without powers) to become public. Parliament agreed this by an Act of 1859, after which it was leased in March 1860 to the NSR and passenger services between Stoke and Silverdale commenced during 1862. On 29th July 1864 Parliament agreed the NSR branch from Silverdale to Market Drayton.

On 1st February 1870 Market Drayton was reached with an official opening for both goods and passenger traffic. This was not the first railway to reach Market Drayton since GWR lines already existed from both Wellington and Nantwich (chapter 11), so celebrations were somewhat muted. In the book *The Stoke to Market Drayton Line*, C R Lester wrote of the various festivities that did take place. A commemorative public ball was held at the Corbet Arms assembly rooms in Market Drayton and, at Pipe Gate, visitors from Silverdale were among the 30 guests who celebrated at the Chetwode Arms Inn with a dinner to mark the occasion. The toast was 'Success to the North Staffordshire Railway' and, when the last train left Pipe Gate for Stoke at 8.35 pm, few were on it. One may assume celebrations lasted well into the night with a number of bleary-eyed passengers on the 10.45 am the next morning.

Four trains ran each way weekdays and two on Sundays with intermediate stations initially between Market Drayton and Silverdale at Norton-in-Hales, Pipe Gate (for Pipe Gate and Woore) and Keele (for Keele and Madeley). As well as providing a useful passenger service plus agricultural links, it was expected the line would further develop collieries plus bring North Staffordshire into direct communication with GWR lines. On the branch, the need for half-day excursions out of Stoke turned Norton-in-Hales into a health resort and it soon became popular with tourists looking for a country outing or as a place for 'Sunday School treats'.

Following the arrival of NSR trains, the original passenger station at Market Drayton was enlarged. It was rebuilt in a 'French Renaissance' style with ornamental ironwork and square-topped pavilions at each end. In later years through trains were operated

Norton-in-Hales station, formerly on the Stoke/Market Drayton branch, is today a private residence. The line closed to passengers in May 1956. (Author)

Market Drayton station c1910. When the North Staffordshire Railway's trains reached the town from Stoke in February 1870, it was initially more an intention to keep the GWR out of the area rather than provide a rail service. (Lens of Sutton)

via Market Drayton on GWR tracks to Hodnet on market days and often further south to places south of Wellington. Madeley station, described as a 'small wayside station', opened later between Keele and Pipe Gate. For a short time during 1871 Madeley station was known as Madeley Manor, later to become Madeley Road for the rest of its life.

Pipe Gate became busy with trade in timber and cattle and in the 1880s a creamery and milk condensing plant was established. Services to Pipe Gate increased considerably when, in 1885, a race course was laid out on farmland about half a mile to the north of the station. Race trains came from many Midlands towns and extra staff were drafted in to cope with the crowds. Towards Stoke a small station called Keele Park was opened when Ralph Sneyd (son of the iron master – another Ralph) constructed a steeple-chase course. Training and breeding stables were set up nearby and a horse loading dock was built at Keele station. The race course lasted until 1901 when Sneyd's family finances deteriorated.

Following the demands of the Silverdale and Apedale coal plants, a system of 'private' working was developed over NSR tracks. For many years a passenger service was provided for employees from Newcastle-under-Lyme to meet the various shifts and the train, usually ex-NSR four-wheeled coaches, became known as the 'Apedale Paddy'. There were numerous stops at places such as Brampton and Liverpool Road (opened 1905) plus other unofficial stops close to pits so that trains were often empty when reaching the Apedale terminus.

In 1905 a Beyer Peacock railcar was introduced to the Market Drayton branch as an economy measure. Many passengers had been lost owing to poverty in the area plus competition from trams. Further halts were opened in an effort to attract passengers but, as the 1920s progressed, competition from road transport took its

toll. When the trams were abandoned in 1928, they were replaced by the Potteries Motor Traction Company which developed a regular service along much of the route. To compete, the NSR (now LMS) provided additional trains but it was in vain. Early in 1956 British Rail announced closure of the line from Market Drayton to Silverdale and, despite efforts by a local Transport Users' Consultative Committee, the end for passenger traffic came on Saturday, 5th May.

As usual for a final day, the train carried its heaviest load for many years. As 2-6-4T locomotive no 42671 hauled four coaches from Market Drayton at 7 pm, the occasion was marked by exploding detonators. Along the line small groups of mourners watched the passing. Eighty-six years of service had come to an end although passenger services between the Silverdale and Stoke section lasted a further eight years until closure on 2nd March 1964.

Today a spur from the main Crewe to Stafford line carries freight trains which then reverse onto a section of the former Market Drayton branch. When the M6 was built in 1961 a single line bridge had to be built to carry the surviving track across the six motor lanes just north of Keele. Keele station has gone but perhaps the name today implies more a motorway service area than a railway station – surely a sad reflection of our changing times.

An early picture of Station Bridge at Audley. The station was originally known as Audley & Bignall End. Although primarily a mineral line, passenger services were provided lasting until 1931. Today only 'Bridge Close' indicates where the station existed. (Photograph by kind permission of the Borough Museum & Art Gallery, Newcastle-under-Lyme)

Keele/Audley/Alsager Road/Harecastle

A mineral line to Alsager from the NSR Market Drayton branch was approved by Parliament on 29th July 1864. It was really more a collection of lines serving busy collieries such as Audley, Bignall Hill, Rookery and Jamage. Construction work was slow, particularly between Silverdale and Leycett, requiring the excavation of a deep cutting followed by a high embankment. This section was beset throughout with problems from flooding and mining subsidence and was abandoned when an alternative route between Honeywall and Leycett became available in 1870.

There were further problems with the many colliery sidings proving sub-standard and it was to be quite a number of years before the Board of Trade approved the line for passenger traffic. Eventually it was agreed the permanent way and the signalling met requirements and passenger services between Stoke and Harecastle commenced on the Audley branch on 28th June 1880. There were four trains each way daily and two on Sundays. Intermediate stations were at Leycett, Halmerend and Audley with the buildings constructed of wood for cheapness. On July 1st 1889 a fourth station opened called 'Talke & Alsager Road' but the name was shortened to Alsager Road in 1902.

The mine owners were not happy with the alternative Honeywall route since this meant extra mileage costs and to partly overcome this the NSR built a short east-facing spur at Honeywall so that trains could avoid reversal and enjoy through running to Stoke. This was opened on 1st October 1880 and the tracks on the western curve were removed.

During the period of depression after the First World War, many of the pits between Talke and Silverdale closed down. This stretch of track had for a time been among the most profitable on the NSR but as the pits became 'worked out' so hardship followed for the many men put out of work. When Talke pit closed in 1928, 1,000 men lost their jobs and in 1930 five more collieries closed down. On 27th April 1931 passenger services came to an end, finally forced to close by competition from buses which proved more convenient. Over the next three decades, freight services survived but they were run down as pits continued to close. For the last two years, only occasional trains reached Audley and none

NSR locomotive no 21 class B leaves Harecastle c1920. Originally built as a 2-4-0T in 1882 at Stoke, it was rebuilt a 2-4-2T in 1901. In 1925 the LMS renumbered the locomotive 1457. (Lens of Sutton)

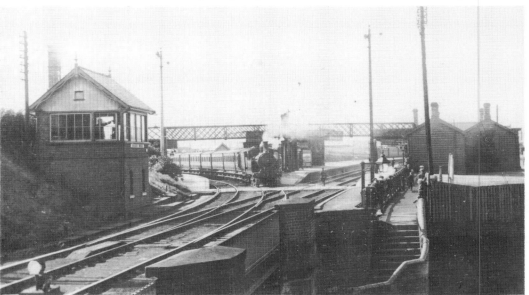

beyond. In September 1957, Madeley Colliery at Leycett closed, the last of the once famous local pits, and by the late 1960s all freight had come to an end.

Harecastle/Sandbach

Although mainly in Cheshire, the short branch emanated from Harecastle in Staffordshire and warrants mention. This NSR line of 6½ miles passing through quiet Cheshire countryside must surely have had the reputation of being one of the country's shortest-lived passenger lines. The Act agreeing the branch was passed by Parliament in 1846 but it was to be another 47 years before it opened throughout to passengers and then it lasted only 37 years. Had it developed further, it could have taken NSR trains closer to Liverpool but as it was, it settled initially for goods traffic only from 1852, between Lawton junction (on the main Crewe/ Stoke line) and Ettiley Heath, a goods depot just short of Sandbach (on the Crewe/Manchester route). When goods services reached Sandbach in 1866, the branch was seen as a useful means to take pressure off some of Crewe's freight traffic.

Passenger services commenced on 3rd July 1893 with intermediate stations at Lawton, Hassall Green and Sandbach (Wheelock), the last renamed 'Wheelock & Sandbach' in 1923. Between Hassall Green and Wheelock a short siding carried freight to and from Malkin's Bank, the vast alkali works of Brunner Mond, the forerunner of ICI. On 28th July 1930 passenger services on the branch came to an end but the line continued usefully carrying freight until the early 1970s as a Crewe avoiding route.

Today Harecastle station is no more. When the route from Euston to the North West was electrified in the 1960s, the nearby tunnels were found to be too narrow for present day stock. One tunnel (Harecastle North) was opened out and two others were

Hassall Green on the Harecastle to Sandbach branch where the station building has become a private residence. The bridge beyond carries the M6 motorway. (Author)

All that is left of Wheelock station where track passed below the A534 Sandbach Road. The station closed to passengers in 1930 but the line survived until the 1970s as a freight 'Crewe-avoiding' line. (Lens of Sutton)

abandoned. British Rail constructed a loop and built Kidsgrove station at a new site (see chapter 13). Hassall Green's former station building exists as a private residence although rather over-shadowed by the M6 motorway. Wheelock station building has become a garage found at the top end of the town whilst the former platform is lost in the wooded glade below.

Two useful contributions to preserved railways came from the branch. The signal box currently in use at the North Staffordshire Railway at Cheddleton came from Elton crossing at Sandbach and the signal box and crossing gates at Hassall Green found their way to Hadlow Road station museum in the Wirral Country Park, on the former Hooton to West Kirby branch.

Chapter 13

STAFFORDSHIRE PIT LINES AND A LOOP
(Stoke-on-Trent/Bucknall/Biddulph/Congleton, Bucknall/
Endon/Leek, Etruria/Tunstall/Kidsgrove)

Stoke-on-Trent/Bucknall/Biddulph/Congleton
A visit to the Chatterley Whitfield Mining Museum can prove an
absorbing experience for young and elderly alike. Opened to the
public in 1979, this was Britain's first underground mining
museum, located on the site of the former million ton per annum
colliery. Since its launch more than half a million people have
enjoyed an exciting journey into the past and present of North
Staffordshire's mining industry.

For railway enthusiasts perhaps the most interesting exhibit to
be found is the NSR tank locomotive no 2 L class 0-6-2T built
at Stoke works in 1921. The locomotive, on loan from the National
Railway Museum, is not currently in working order and it is
estimated that restoration costs could amount to as much as
£100,000. The Chatterley Whitfield Railway Society, worked
entirely by volunteers, does not lack enthusiasm. There are hopes
to eventually extend the existing half mile of (non-passenger
carrying) track to the main road making one mile in all.

Stoke developed a national reputation for the excellence of its
pottery in the 19th century although the manufacturing process
was far cruder and more wasteful than in today's kilns. For each
ton of clay about ten tons of coal was needed for the firing of
products. Thus the siting of the Potteries, in an age of primitive
transport, owed as much to the presence of nearby pits as to local
clays. The area has its origins in numerous communities which

*Stoke Station Square
c1910. NSR trains first
came to Stoke in April
1848 when a temporary
station opened providing a
service to Norton Bridge
giving a link with
Birmingham and London.
(Photograph courtesy City
Central Library, Hanley)*

Congleton station c1905 looking northwards. The signal box carried a sign Telegrams, a facility available at the station. (Lens of Sutton)

together gave plentiful employment. In the 1920s, for example, more than 4,500 men worked at Chatterley Whitfield Colliery alone. Such was the power wielded by the colliery owners that they could compel smaller railway companies to build lines to carry their products where needed and, if the railway companies declined, they said they would build a railway themselves. It was in such circumstances that the Potteries, Biddulph and Congleton Railway was conceived and, when the railway company went ahead, it had to carry all the colliery's expenses!

The Biddulph Valley line from Stoke to a terminal at Congleton was agreed by Parliament on 24th July 1854. The NSR accepted a tender of £87,500 submitted by William and Solomon Tredwell and the first sod was cut on 27th April 1858. Since the movement of coal was the line's greatest priority, it commenced initially for goods only on 29th August 1860. Passenger services began on 1st June 1864, when the *Macclesfield Courier* reported, 'The first passenger train left Stoke at 8.45 am, the engine driver having decorated his iron horse with oak and laburnum, interspersed with a few flags emblazoned with the Staffordshire Knot'.

As expected, the line was busiest with mineral traffic. With Whitfield Colliery producing near to a million tons annually by 1900 (it reached its first million in 1937), and with other collieries along the branch such as Northwood or Birchenwood, the line could not fail. Originally coal trains from the Chatterley Whitfield colliery joined the branch near Black Bull but when the Potteries Loop line was built, the colliery built its own system, the Whitfield Colliery Railway, joining the Loop south of Tunstall. This spur to Tunstall became known as the Pinnox branch.

Travelling the Biddulph Valley branch from Stoke, tracks left the main Stoke-Derby line to curve northwards to Fenton Manor which was opened later in October 1889. Originally a wooden platform, a brick extension was added in May 1892. At Botteslow junction, the Longton, Adderley Green & Bucknall Railway left the main branch diverging to the east. This was a little known but busy mineral line sanctioned in 1866 to reach Longton plus two pit branches. It was later extended to Park Hall on the main Stoke/ Uttoxeter line to become a circular route. When taken over by the NSR in May 1895, the line was immediately cut in two by the abandonment of a ¼ mile stretch close to the southern end. This was done partly to simplify working and also to benefit the NSR by increasing revenue from the longer hauls required. Even though powers were granted to run passenger trains, this never happened.

Back to the Biddulph line and not far from Northwood colliery came Bucknall & Northwood station. A mile or so further north at Milton junction, trains left for Leek and Waterhouses. Before Ford Green & Smallthorne station the track was crossed by a mineral line between Nettlebank Wharf and Ford Green iron-works. In 1890 Chatterley Whitfield introduced its own workmen's train with services started from the pit yard. After Black Bull station and a private spur to Birchenwood colliery came Knypersley Halt. The name Knypersley means 'the village under the rocks' and near the busy cross-roads stands the parish church of St John, donated by the Bateman family as well as coal owners and industrialists from the last century. Beyond Biddulph and Mossley halt, the branch passed under the main line (Congleton to Macclesfield) to its terminus at Congleton, with a spur climbing to join the main route.

When the London, Midland & Scottish Railway (LMS) took over after grouping in the early 1920s, the Biddulph branch was one of the first to suffer. The LMS thought the line had no future for passenger traffic and regular Stoke/Congleton services ended on 11th July 1927. Another factor which contributed to passenger loss was the LMS policy of not allowing private trains over its lines.

The remains of Endon station between Milton junction and Leek, May 1992. After closure to passengers in 1956, the line remained open for goods but today it is no longer in use. (Author)

Mineral traffic continued healthily for many years even though the industry was in decline. In 1963 the branch lost its spur at Congleton to the main line and the following year the Pinnox line closed when a new connection to the Biddulph line was installed. Further closures followed in 1968 when the line north of Biddulph closed and in 1976 between Ford Green and Biddulph (Victoria colliery). When the section between Ford Green and Milton junction went, only the line from Stoke to Milton junction survived, providing freight services beyond via Leek to Oakamoor and Caldon Low.

Bucknall/Endon/Leek

The Milton junction/Leek Brook stretch, agreed by Parliament on 13th July 1863, was single track and over six miles in length. There were delays in completion since considerable earthworks were necessary and there were also difficulties in raising the necessary finance. Over four years after authorisation, on 1st November 1867, the line finally opened to both passenger and freight traffic.

There were intermediate stations at Milton, Stockton Brook, Endon and Wall Grange. At Stockton Brook the railway line still passes diagonally under a crossroad which includes the busy A53 from Stoke to Leek. The next stop eastwards was Endon where the platform has survived, a shop standing today on the site of the platform building. A section of the Caldon Canal passes Endon but at a height of 490 feet above sea level. Built by James Brindley in 1777, it is believed to be the highest canal in Britain. It is no longer used commercially but following restoration by the Caldon Canal Society and British Waterways, it brings much pleasure as a Leisure Cruiseway.

The railway lasted until 7th May 1956 when passenger services

Wall Grange, an intermediate station between Endon and Leek. In the foreground is the Caldon Canal. (Photograph by kind permission of the Borough Museum & Art Gallery, Newcastle-under-Lyme)

from Stoke to Leek were withdrawn. The line remained in use for goods, linking Stoke with Oakamoor and Caldon Low and, for a time from 1956 to 1960, the branch was used by football specials. Although the track remains today, it is no longer in use. The days of travelling by train to Stoke have been truly forgotten.

A recollection of the former Loop Line. Driving wheels (class 5 standard) set in concrete, can be found today at Pitts Hill on the pathway known as the Potteries Greenway. (Author)

Etruria/Tunstall/Kidsgrove

'The formal death announcement of the historic Potteries Loop Line passenger service was issued by British Railways today. Only the date of the execution – method the Beeching Axe – remains to be fixed'. The above statement headed a newspaper feature in January 1964. Another reported, 'The death knell sounded for the line some time ago and many of its daytime services have already been suspended. But when the Minister's official approval of the closure came last week, it caused bitterness and strong protests among the many regulars who use the half-a-dozen daily trains'. The Potteries Loop Line always had a place in NSR ('Knotty') supporters' hearts and such was the reaction locally when the London Midland Region headquarters at Birmingham announced its closure.

To go back to its beginning, several Acts required Parliamentary approval before the Loop Line through the heavily populated and industrial areas to the east of Stoke could be completed. A goods line had already reached Hanley in December 1861 and it was to be another four years before the NSR received approval to complete the line from Hanley via Burslem and Tunstall to Kidsgrove. Meantime industry had slumped and the NSR was anxious to abandon the idea. Local feeling in favour of the line ran high and an approach by the NSR to Parliament to give up the Loop was

Locomotive NSR class L 0-6-2T no 2 preserved at the Chatterley Whitfield Mining Museum. Built at Stoke Works in 1921, it is not currently in working order and funds to restore are much needed. (Courtesy Staffordshire County Museum, Shugborough)

rejected. To cut costs the NSR investigated a narrow gauge system but this proposal was thrown out by shareholders.

Construction went ahead with the first sod cut on 21st July 1870 at Burslem with John Watkin, the town's Chief Bailiff, officiating. In the book *The Potteries Loop line*, Allan C Baker wrote that much celebration followed and the guests, no doubt accompanied by many others, repaired to the Leopard Hotel for suitable refreshments. By all accounts a good time was had by all. Over five years later, on 15th November 1875, the Loop Line finally opened as a through route from Etruria to Kidsgrove. *The Staffordshire Daily Sentinel* reported 'There was a great stir in consequence of the opening of this line, so much so, that it was observed to be very much like the Wakes and many of the pits were idle. The first two trains were very much crowded, while a still greater number surrounded the entrance to (Kidsgrove) station'.

The first full passenger service came into operation in December 1875 with as many as 25 trains each way on weekdays from Tunstall southwards via Stoke to Longton or Blythe Bridge. Initially only a few trains travelled northwards from Tunstall towards Kidsgrove where demand was less. The Loop Line became known as the 'inner circle' of the Potteries and with trains every half hour, the NSR, despite its earlier forebodings, found the branch very profitable. The trains, mostly older four-wheeled coaches hauled by 2-4-0 side tank locomotives known as 'Sharp Tanks' carried special name boards with 'Loop Line Train' in black letters on a white background. After a few years some of the four-wheeled coaches were replaced by six-wheeled carriages.

In 1909 a halt was opened at Kidsgrove to encourage traffic, to be known as Market Street Halt. A disadvantage for Loop traffic was the lack of any direct connection with Harecastle station on the main Stoke/Macclesfield line. When trains at the northern end of the Loop joined the main Macclesfield line they were beyond Harecastle station and facing the wrong direction. Plans were considered to overcome this but nothing was ever done.

On 1st July 1923 the NSR became part of the London, Midland & Scottish Railway (LMS). Changes were inevitable particularly with competition from trams and buses already affecting Loop traffic. Even so by the late 1920s, there were still some 20 trains daily between Tunstall and Stoke. Some extended northwards to terminate at either Kidsgrove or Congleton while southwards, trains went to Blythe Bridge, Cheadle or Uttoxeter. Just prior to the Second World War some Sunday trains ran to and from Trentham Park, a terminus on a short one-mile branch close to Trentham Gardens (chapter 14). In October 1944 Harecastle station on the main line was renamed Kidsgrove Central and Kidsgrove station on the loop became Kidsgrove London Road. After closure of the loop Kidsgrove Central became just Kidsgrove.

As pits closed over the years that followed, freight traffic reduced considerably. Closure to passenger services came on 2nd March 1964 although short sections survived for a number of years for freight purposes. Meantime electrification of the main line between Euston and the North West was in hand and a Harecastle tunnel diversion line was opened on 27th June 1966. This was necessary because the original main line tunnels were too narrow for the new trains. Harecastle North tunnel (130 yds) was opened out and the Middle (180 yds) and South (1,763 yds) tunnels were abandoned. Today only a 220 yd tunnel is required. When a full electric service began on 2nd January 1967, track lifting along the Loop was put in hand.

When electrification of the main line between Euston and the North West was completed in 1966/67, a diversion line was opened bypassing Harecastle's earlier three tunnels. This former tunnel, photographed in 1967, has now been demolished. (Courtesy Staffordshire County Museum, Shugborough)

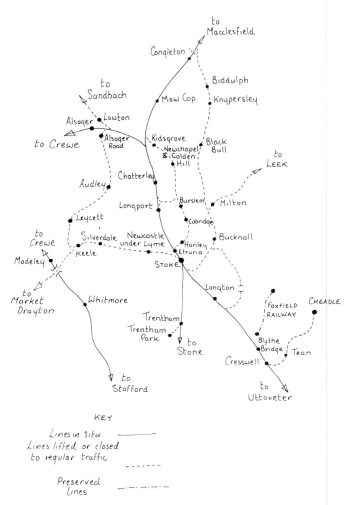

to
Macclesfield

Congleton

Biddulph
Mow Cop   Knypersley
to
Sandbach

Alsager Lawton
Alsager   Kidsgrove
to Crewe   Road   Black
Newchapel   Bull
& Golden
Hill

Chatterley
Audley

Longport   Burslem   Milton

Leycett   Cobridge
to
Crewe   Silverdale Newcastle
under Lyme   Hanley   Bucknall
Keele   Etruria
Madeley   STOKE
to
Market   Whitmore   Longton
Drayton   FOXFIELD   CHEADLE
RAILWAY
Trentham
Trentham   Blythe
Park   to   Bridge   Tean
Stone   Cresswell
to   to
Stafford   Uttoxeter

to
LEEK

KEY

Lines in situ ————

Lines lifted or closed
to regular traffic ········

Preserved
lines ·—·—·—·—

After more than a century the Loop Line may be no more but it is still remembered by many. Today much of the track has become a pathway known as the *Loop Greenway*. At the site where the Pitt's Hill section was opened in 1972, a set of class 5 standard driving wheels have been set in a concrete bed and at Burslem the smokebox from GWR no 3817 class 28XX can be seen from the A50. When visited by the author early in May 1992 the latter area was being developed as a leisure complex and the smokebox lay ignominiously on its side. It began its life at Swindon – but what a sad ending!

Chapter 14

A RESTORED COLLIERY LINE, TWO BRANCHES AND AN INTERESTING PUBLIC HOUSE

(The Foxfield Steam Railway, Cresswell/Cheadle, Trentham/
Trentham Park and The Spot Gate Inn, near Stone)

The Foxfield Steam Railway
A visit to the Foxfield Steam Railway at Blythe Bridge can also be
a trip back into history. In the late 1880s a shaft was sunk in
Foxfield Wood and the resultant colliery was named after it.
Initially most of the coal was taken by narrow gauge railway to the
outskirts of Cheadle but, as coal production increased, a standard
gauge freight line was built to connect with the NSR line at Blythe
Bridge. The line was built with the minimum of earthworks hence
the steep gradients and sharp curves found at the Foxfield today.

When the colliery closed in August 1965 the site was purchased
by a consortium of local companies with plans to process various
minerals for the nearby pottery industry and it was expected that
the rail link to the BR line at Blythe Bridge would prove useful.
This did not happen but fortunately some of the directors of one
of the companies, Tean Minerals Ltd., showed interest in preserv-
ing the line. In 1967 the Foxfield Light Railway was formed and
Tean Minerals generously gave the society unrestricted use of the
line plus certain of the buildings and sidings.

Today the enthusiasm of volunteers at Foxfield is hard to match.
Trains run from Caverswall Road station to Dilhorne Park and
back and there are hopes that in the distant future trains may
operate the full length of the original track. Relics from earlier

*Ex-NCB NW area 0-6-0
Hunslet in steam at
Caverswall Road station
on the Foxfield Steam
Railway on 10th May
1992. Built at Leeds in
1950, the Hunslet worked
at Lancashire collieries for
a number of years.
(Author)*

NSR workers (and a dog!) pose at Blythe Bridge station during the First World War 1914–1918. (Courtesy Staffordshire County Museum, Shugborough)

days can also be found. In Caverswall Road station building, parts of the wooden booking office originally came from Gnosall, formerly on the Wellington to Stafford line. A signal box came from Ford Green on the Biddulph Valley line some years ago to reside at Dilhorne Park but sadly, after continual and systematic vandalism, this had to be demolished.

Steam-hauled trains provide a regular service from Caverswall Road on Sundays and Bank Holidays from Easter to the end of September when it is possible to enjoy a five mile journey through unspoilt countryside. Plans are in hand at present to add sidings as well as construct a building to house the fine array of locomotives and railway stock accumulated. Unfortunately many of these had to be delivered by road transport since in the mid-1970s BR, for reasons best known to itself, removed the connection with the main line.

When the author visited Foxfield in May 1992, he was privileged to have a footplate ride on steam powered 0-6-0 Hunslet, works

Tean station c1910 on the Cheadle branch looking towards Cresswell in busier times! Prior to 1906, the station was called Totmonslow. (Lens of Sutton)

Only the platform edge has survived at the site of Tean station. The track is lost in undergrowth and is no longer used. (Author)

no 3694. Acquired by its present owner, Steve Turner, in 1983 after working Lancashire collieries, it has seen many travels. After 'Crewe 150' in 1987 it was loaned to Swanage Railway during much of 1990. When the author rejoined his wife afterwards, herself a rail enthusiast some of the time, instead of acclamations of praise and envy, her only comment was, 'Your hands are dirty!'

Cresswell/Cheadle

There were great celebrations when a crowded first train left Totmonslow (Tean from December 1906) via Cresswell for Tunstall on the Potteries Loop line on 7th November 1892. Hauled by an NSR tank locomotive, Cheadle branch trains were to become an extension of Loop line services. But the celebrations could be considered somewhat premature for another eight years were to pass before trains actually reached Cheadle.

A branch to Cheadle was first considered in the early 1850s when the local people felt they had been neglected by the Stoke-Uttoxeter and the Churnet Valley lines which passed nearly four miles each side of the town. Various ideas were proposed and rejected and it was not until August 1888 that Parliament agreed a line. The townsfolk of Cheadle, having waited so many years, were impatient to get their railway and the first sod was cut on 22nd March 1888, five months before the Bill was passed.

Many problems were to follow before the line was completed. As the company ran out of money, so work stopped. In addition a costly tunnel 977 yards long was required with gradients reaching 1 in 40. Trains eventually reached Cheadle on 1st January 1901, 13 years after Parliamentary approval had been given. There were five trains each way daily and two on Sundays, still an extension of the Loop line traffic. Freight traffic was spasmodic, dependent on the output of the two collieries, Draycott and New Haden, along the route. Almost from the start there was a problem with the tunnel when part of the lining collapsed and repairs proved a heavy expense. When the two collieries closed during 1906, finances further deteriorated and the Cheadle Railway Company went into liquidation.

Matters improved when the NSR took over in 1907. Services increased, the New Haden colliery re-opened under new owner- ship and Tean acquired a more permanent station building. Pas- sengers had to wait another two years before toilets were opened! A cottage near the station served as a booking office, a building which survives today as a private residence. At Cheadle a large new

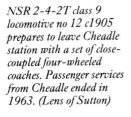

NSR 2-4-2T class 9 locomotive no 12 c1905 prepares to leave Cheadle station with a set of close- coupled four-wheeled coaches. Passenger services from Cheadle ended in 1963. (Lens of Sutton)

station with an awning was built plus a large house for the station master. This awning would have proved useful at Foxfield's Caverswall Road station but BR demolished it along with the station after closure.

Troubles with the tunnel persisted, much of it caused by the New Haden colliery workings. Events took a dramatic turn on Sunday afternoon 2nd November 1918 when 400 ft of the tunnel

roof at the Cheadle end collapsed, completely blocking the line. Fortunately no trains were running at the time and traffic was suspended for several weeks while extensive repairs were carried out.

When in 1923 the LMS took over control of the NSR and with it the Cheadle branch, it also inherited the continuing tunnel problem. Troubles persisted and in 1931 Parliament agreed that a diversion line could be built skirting the high ground. Work began in 1932 which included the removal of some 145,000 cubic yards of earth. Finally after over 30 years of problems the new line was opened on 26th November 1933. In his book *The Cheadle Railway*, Allan C. Baker rightly asks why was the line not initially built to skirt the high ground? How too could the LMS justify such a heavy financial outlay on a relatively unimportant branch?

Traffic declined during the Second World War with further losses in 1943 when New Haden colliery closed. There was some compensation when a small brickworks was installed near the colliery site providing useful goods traffic for the movement of staple sand. Nationalisation followed in 1948 and in 1953 Tean station closed through lack of use. Despite falling traffic generally, passenger traffic survived until 1963. The last train, the 5.07 pm from Cheadle, ran on Saturday, 17th June 1963. Fifteen years later public freight workings were withdrawn.

Cheadle station site can be found along Station Road. The platform edge can be determined and the station master's house is a private residence. At the end of the former track, buffers stand isolated. Tean platform is still there overlooking overgrown and neglected track. It can be seen from the bridge on the minor road from Upper Tean to Longton. But no trains pass – only the ghosts of ex-LMS class 5 or class 8 or perhaps an Ivatt 2-6-0 might be heard.

The unusual Italianate style of Trentham station on the Stoke to Stone main line. In 1910 the NSR opened a 1¼ mile branch to Trentham Gardens which lasted until 1939 for regular passenger traffic. (Lens of Sutton)

Inside one of the Pullman cars at the Spot Gate pub (east of Stone) where meals are served to a high standard in highly evocative surroundings. The pub's coaches were built at Birmingham in 1928. (Author)

Trentham/Trentham Park

The 1,000 acres of Trentham Gardens to the south of Stoke-on-Trent have a long and colourful history dating back to Saxon times. During the 19th century the estate was the ancestral home of the Dukes of Sutherland. Today the area offers a wide range of activities ranging from clay pigeon shooting or water skiing, to a wildfowl reserve or a children's funfair. Also included is a minia-ture railway but it was standard gauge trains that travelled the 1¼ mile branch which opened to the gardens in April 1910.

Even though Trentham Gardens were within walking distance from the main line station of Trentham, the NSR decision to build this short branch justified itself. But plans to extend by construct-ing the Trentham, Newcastle-under-Lyme and Silverdale Railway to form a western outer circle around Stoke came to nothing when the First World War broke out in 1914. All that was built was a steel girder bridge on high brick abutments (all now demolished) beyond the Trentham Gardens terminus over the A34.

The branch had only one intermediate stop at Hanford Road Halt, today hardly a rural area. The halt closed in 1913 but the branch itself lasted until a few days after the Second World War began, closing to regular passenger traffic on 11th September 1939. Excursion traffic continued for a time but the line closed completely in October 1957.

The Spot Gate Inn, near Stone

Interesting railway relics can be found at The Spot Gate public house to the north of Hilderstone and near Stone where two

96

'retired' coaches form the popular Pullman Restaurant. The coaches have quite a history with one named *Ursula*, a parlour 1st class, being one of 30 made to introduce the *Queen of Scots* service remaining with the London & North Eastern Railway (LNER) until the early 1960s. After service with the *Bournemouth Belle*, it was withdrawn in 1967.

The second coach had the added distinction that it worked with the *Golden Arrow* in 1960 as well as the *Bournemouth Belle* from 1965 to 1967. Both were built by the Metropolitan Carriage Wagon & Finance Co., of Saltley, Birmingham in 1928 and after withdrawal were sold to Allied Breweries. Today it is possible to enjoy a fine meal in either coach and, at the same time, capture much of the railway spirit of the past.

Chapter 15

THE CHURNET VALLEY BRANCH, A LINE INTO DERBYSHIRE AND STEAM AT CHEDDLETON

(Uttoxeter/Leek/North Rode, Rocester/Ashbourne, The Cheddleton Railway Centre)

Uttoxeter/Leek/North Rode

The North Staffordshire Railway (NSR) line from Uttoxeter to North Rode could well have achieved far greater importance for it provided the shortest distance between Euston and Manchester. Although used by some through services, most of the trains ran via Stoke or Crewe. When it opened on 13th July 1849, there were initially four trains each way daily with two on Sundays but equally important was the branch's freight traffic. Milk from the Churnet, Dane and Dove areas left regularly for London or Manchester and copper transported from Oakamoor and later from Froghall proved profitable.

Powers to build the Churnet Valley Railway were granted in 1846. At the time three companies were planning lines in Staffordshire: the Potteries, the Harecastle & Sandbach and the Churnet Valley. These combined in 1847 to become the North Staffordshire Railway. Although the Churnet Valley branch was completed in three years, it was not easy to construct. Part of the track between Froghall and Uttoxeter had to be laid on a drained canal and in addition four tunnels had to be bored. Leek and Alton were considered to be the main intermediate stations and the 'clerks' in charge received a higher salary than their colleagues at the lesser stops. In an NSR Rule Book of the day, staff were expected to

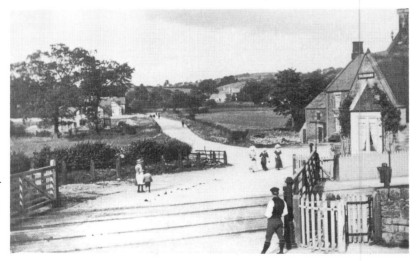

The level crossing at Rushton on the Churnet Valley branch c1910. The station closed in November 1960 and the track has gone. (Photograph by kind permission of the Borough Museum & Art Gallery, Newcastle-under-Lyme)

Rushton station building, photographed in May 1992 and now a private residence. Although closed to passenger traffic in 1960, a notice still reminds passers-by to BEWARE OF TRAINS. (Author)

ensure that 'all servants came on duty clean in their persons and their clothes, shaved and with their shoes blacked'. Later the shaving rule was relaxed for engine drivers who were allowed to grow beards, presumably to serve as chest protectors!

Travelling southwards from North Rode, the line passed through pleasant countryside to reach Bosley, a timber-style station set in a cutting. Next came Rushton where the station building survives today as an attractive private residence. A prominent notice on the wall reads BEWARE OF TRAINS. Rudyard Lake station (opened in 1905) came next, known as Cliffe Park from 1926. The lake was created as a reservoir for the Caldon Canal and it was at this lakeside that Stoke architect Kipling proposed to Rudyard Kipling's mother. The lake also later gave the famous novelist and poet his name.

At the south end of the lake came Rudyard (Horton) station which was known as Rudyard Lake prior to 1905. It seems hard to believe that not too many years ago on Bank Holidays, trains ran from Leek to Rudyard and back every quarter of an hour. Leek was reached after crossing the river Churnet and passing through the 462 yd Leek Tunnel. Today all trace of the station has gone and the site is occupied by a supermarket. To the south was Leek Brook Halt, opened at the turn of the century to serve a newly built mental hospital. The halt had one platform plus a bay which accommodated an electrically powered branch to the hospital for freight and visitors although later it was for freight only.

Cheddleton station, sited some way from the village of the same name, possessed a small siding hardly adequate to cope with the output of a nearby paper mill. Consall opened in 1902 serving a small community, followed by Kingsley & Froghall, which became an important rail point. Nearby was the terminus of the Caldon Canal and the tramway from the Caldon Quarries. In the book *The Churnet Valley Railway*, R Keys writes that a signal box just to the north of Kingsley & Froghall station was staffed for many years by

Leek station and yard around the turn of the century. The station closed to passengers in 1970 and was demolished in 1973/ 4. The goods shed on the right survived until around 1989. (Lens of Sutton)

an unfortunate fellow who lost both legs when he was run over by a train. The NSR provided him with wooden stumps and kept him in his employment where he became affectionately known as 'Peg-Leg' Johnson.

Oakamoor gained its reputation from the local industries sited in the area. One of the most important was the copper business of Thomas Bolton & Sons which produced the first successful trans-atlantic cable. To the south, Alton station building survives today as a listed building, built in a style to match Alton Towers, former home of the Earl of Shrewsbury. Situated on the steep side of the Churnet Valley, the station had a luggage lift to hoist the earl's belongings up to his front entrance. Excursion trains to Alton were many and a long bay platform coped with the busy traffic. In the 1920s Alton Towers estate was sold to a local consortium which opened a pleasure park, a feature that very much remains today.

The last intermediate station before Rocester was Denstone, built originally to serve the Heywood family who lived in what became Denstone College. It had a very low platform and passen-gers had to alight down small step ladders provided for the purpose. At Rocester the branch joined the line from Ashbourne, thus completing almost 28 miles of delightful scenery. The site of Rocester station has become the vast JCB excavator works and some locals have claimed that at night 'ghosts trains' can still be heard in the factory buildings.

The North Rode to Leek section closed to passengers in November 1960 and Leek to Uttoxeter followed in January 1965. Freight continued for a time but in November 1992 even the lines which still exist from Stoke via Leek Brook junction to Oakamoor and Caldon Low were no longer in use. Is it possible perhaps that, when our economic climate improves, Tarmac or Redland freight trains may travel the line again?

Looking back, it seems incredible that in 1973 Leek Urban Council failed to see any potential in bringing steam back between Leek and Rudyard Lake despite petitions from many Leek resi-

dents for the line to be preserved. It seems even more incredible that at the present time, a town the size of Leek, has no railway at all!

In 1985 trains did return to Rudyard but with a 10¼ in gauge layout along part of the former trackbed. Services run most summer weekends and occasionally weekdays during school holidays. The privately owned system includes three locomotives, *Kingsley*, an 0-4-0 diesel powered, an 0-4-0 petrol engine and *Ivanhoe*, a 4-4-0 steam, as well as numerous open bogie coaches.

All is not lost it seems for part of the Churnet Valley line! Consultants have suggested there is potential in re-opening the existing track from Stoke, via Leek, to Oakamoor and providing an extension to Alton which would serve the leisure park. Not only would a commuter service to the area have good prospects but it would also prove quite a bonus for the present-day Cheddleton Railway Centre along its route.

Alton station, renamed Alton Towers in 1954. Used by the Earl of Shrewsbury, the station had a goods lift to raise the Earl's luggage. It can be seen behind the station awning on the right. (Courtesy Staffordshire County Museum, Shugborough)

Rocester/Ashbourne

The seven mile NSR branch from Rocester to Ashbourne in Derbyshire, which opened in 1852, carried little traffic although this much improved when the LNWR opened its branch from Buxton to Ashbourne in 1899, nearly 50 years later. The through route now possible was considered as yet another alternative for services from Euston to Manchester but this did not happen since the mileage was 194 compared with 183½ via Crewe. The branch was never brought up to main-line standard even though the NSR section was doubled when LNWR services from Buxton began.

A day or so before the LNWR line opened, the villagers of Hartington in Derbyshire were given free rides to Ashbourne, many of them never having travelled on a train before. For many people, particularly in bad weather, the branch became a lifeline, for when road traffic came to a standstill, the trains usually got through. Ashbourne's first station, built by the NSR in 1852, was a fine stately building of brick and stone. When the LNWR branch

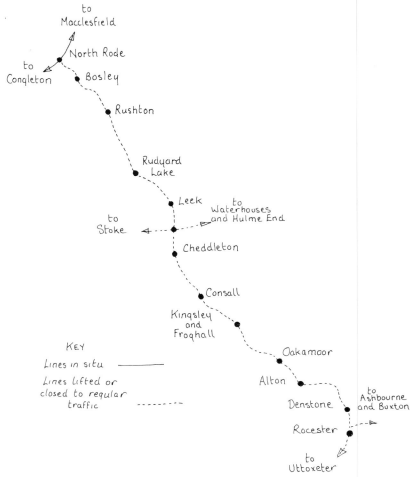

from Buxton arrived, it was relegated to become part of the goods depot with the new Ashbourne station almost entirely wooden. The platforms consisted of planking which passengers found dangerous when wet.

The NSR branch's two intermediate stations were at Norbury & Ellaston and at Clifton with the track following the attractive Dove Valley along the Derbyshire border. There were four trains each way daily on weekdays, two of these later carrying through coaches to Buxton. As rail traffic dwindled in the early 1950s, a typical through train would be a couple of non-corridor coaches hauled by an LMS 2-6-4 tank locomotive. The villagers liked their railway and when closure was threatened local people demanded it should continue. The entire line closed officially to passengers on 1st November 1954 but emergency winter services were continued for a number of years.

The line finally closed to all traffic in June 1964 and the track was removed the same year. During demolition a number of wagons broke loose, to run away smashing three sets of level crossing gates almost as if in protest at the closure. Norbury & Ellaston station building is today a private residence. When visited

102

by the author in May 1992, the owner recalled how he and his wife travelled on the last steam and the last diesel train to Ashbourne. In the past the station had won 'best awards' for appearance, a tradition not neglected by the present owner who, despite near-blindness, kept the garden in very good order. At Clifton, houses have been built across the former track and at Ashbourne the station gave way to become a swimming pool.

The Cheddleton Railway Centre

In May 1974 a parish councillor passed the former Cheddleton station on his way to work and happened to notice that demolition work was in hand. Hurried negotiations with the County Council followed, with the result that the building was saved and the way became clear for the newly-formed volunteer-run North Staffordshire Railway Society, currently known as the North Staffordshire Railway Company (1978) Ltd, to establish the buildings as a headquarters and museum.

Cheddleton station, built 1847 and opened 1849, stands on the now-disused Leek Brook to Oakamoor freight line. While this line now remains silent, the Cheddleton Railway Centre has by contrast gone from strength to strength. When visited by the author in May 1992, all was activity. LMS class 4F 0-6-0 no 4422, rescued from the Barry Scrapyard in 1977, was in full steam hauling two coaches carrying many fascinated visitors. The engine had served much of its time in the south-west including a period in the 1950s on the much-loved former Somerset and Dorset line.

Further steam locomotives at Cheddleton include BR 2-6-4T class 4MT no 80136 built at Brighton in 1956, also rescued from Barry and currently undergoing restoration. There are also two diesel locomotives, one being a new arrival, *Tamworth Castle*, a class 25 built at Derby in 1967 and withdrawn in 1991. Numerous coaches can be seen including 8 ex-BR Mk 1 coaches, an LMS 6-wheel coach and an NSR coach body. The freight stock

Rocester station c1914 when trains were busy and milk travelled by rail. The station nameboard reads 'Change here for Ashbourne and Buxton line'. (Courtesy Staffordshire County Museum, Shugborough)

Ex-LMS class 4F 0-6-0 no 4422 with ex-BR coaches at Cheddleton in May 1992. The locomotive was rescued from Barry scrapyard in 1977 and restored by volunteers. (Author)

comprises mostly LMS/BR wagons or box vans.

The NSR signal box came from Elton Crossing, near Sandbach, and an unrestored example is the former Clifton Crossing box. The former weighbridge office still stands and the NSR Silverdale waiting room shelter has been relocated – brick by brick. The finest modern building is the 3-road brick locomotive display hall only recently added to the Railway Centre.

Future prospects for Cheddleton look good. With the adjacent freight line not at present in use, there is an opportunity for the society to bid for purchase of a seven mile stretch through the selling of shares in the 'Churnet Valley Railway' plc, thus providing the possibility of a northern terminus at Leek Brook (which connects with BR tracks) and a southern terminus at Froghall. Volunteers or 'armchair' members are welcome to help restore this part of 'Owd Knotty'.

Chapter 16

A BRANCH TO WATERHOUSES AND NARROW GAUGE UP THE MANIFOLD VALLEY

(Leek/Waterhouses, Waterhouses/Hulme End)

Leek/Waterhouses

According to the *Leek Post and Times*, a dance was held in a large tent at Waterhouses on Tuesday, 3rd October 1899. The tickets were 6d (2½p) each and it was expected that it would be 'lighted throughout by the New Acetylene Gas'. The occasion formed part of the programme to celebrate the cutting of the first sod for the Leek, Caldon & Waterhouses Railway. Earlier in the day, His Grace the Duke of Devonshire K.G. had honoured the occasion and during the ceremony a special wheelbarrow and spade were presented. A public luncheon followed with tickets at 2s 6d (12½p) each.

Construction of the NSR standard gauge Waterhouses branch met many difficulties. The delays were unfortunate since the Leek & Manifold Valley Light Railway (L&MVLR) opened in June 1904 and the NSR found it necessary to acquire a bus to temporarily connect Leek and Waterhouses until its line was ready. The bus was steam operated having been purchased from Strakers for £700.

There was concern from Leek traders when the NSR planned that a curve at Leek Brook would allow branch trains to run directly to Stoke via Endon joining the Biddulph Valley line at

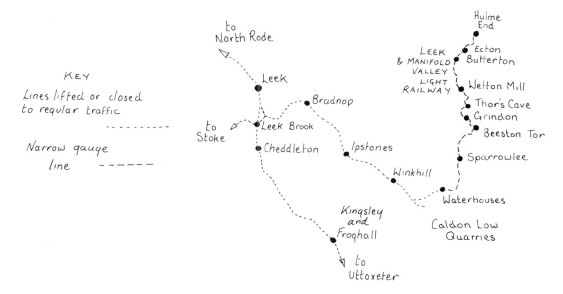

Leek station looking north, taken from under the A53 Leek – Newcastle road. This section has now been infilled although the tunnel has survived. (Lens of Sutton)

The former North Staffordshire Railway goods shed at Waterhouses is today a cycle store from where customers may visit the attractive Manifold Valley. The earlier NSR station has gone. (Author)

Milton junction. Trains to Leek would require a reversal but, following vigorous protests, the NSR was compelled to get Parliamentary approval for a ¼-mile north facing curve. This was completed on 15th June 1905, the same day trains from Leek Brook reached Ipstones.

Despite appalling weather, a number of people turned out at Waterhouses when the village was eventually reached on 1st July 1905. Everywhere was decorated with flags and evergreen to mark the event despite the fact that the station was not yet complete. Initially three trains ran each way daily comprising mixed passenger and goods and linking with trains on the L&MVLR. Passengers could now travel directly by rail from Leek or Stoke, via Leek Brook Junction to the Manifold Valley.

Freight traffic from Caldon Quarry began in July 1906 and became an important feature of the branch with limestone workings beginning in earnest in December 1909. Previously this had been carried by an NSR narrow gauge tramway to Froghall on the

Churnet Valley line and for a time this arrangement continued. Aware of the new standard gauge service, a further quarry face was opened at Caldon requiring almost four tons of gunpowder to release some 45,000 tons of limestone.

Between Leek Brook junction and Waterhouses, principal intermediate stations were at Bradnop and Ipstones with halts at Winkhill and Caldon Low. All were some distance from the villages they claimed to serve and as a result passenger traffic was low. By the 1920s the number of passengers had reduced even further and there was no surprise when services ended on 30th September 1935 with hardly a protest. Freight trains to Waterhouses continued for a further eight years with Stanier class 5 4-6-0s or class 8 2-8-0s a familiar sight. After closure, the line to Caldon Quarry remained open for mineral traffic but today it is no longer in use.

With the track still in situ, the line was easy to trace by the author in 1992. Ipstones station building had gone but the broken-up platform edge had survived. At Winkhill, the platform building has become a private residence. Perhaps the most nostalgic find was near the end of the quarry line at Caldon where a weigh plate house still existed by the track. A fading notice read, 'Drivers must not back their train over the weighbridge plate'.

An NSR class B 2-4-0T locomotive with an inspection saloon waits at the standard gauge Waterhouses station, c1905. In the foreground stands the Leek & Manifold Railway waiting shelter. (Lens of Sutton)

Waterhouses/Hulme End

The former trackbed of the Leek & Manifold Valley Light Railway (L&MVLR) is today a made-up footpath and, should you wish to cycle its length, then you could well be hiring your bicycle from

Leek & Manifold Railway locomotive 2-6-4T no 2 J B Earle in unlined LMS black. The 'colonial' appearance came about because Kitsons had earlier built locomotives for the Barsi Railway in India and the design was copied. (Lens of Sutton)

what was once the NSR goods shed at Waterhouses. The nearby passenger station has long since been demolished but the timber goods shed, which came from Fenton station in 1906, survives as a shop and cycle-hire point. Another distinctive reminder of the past is 164 yard long Swainsley Tunnel to the south of Butterton. Today used by single line motor traffic, it is said this was built at the insistence of Sir Thomas Wardle, a L&MVLR director, so that the view from nearby Swainsley Hall should not be spoilt.

A further tangible reminder of the L&MVLR is at the northern terminus, Hulme End, where the former locomotive shed became part of a council maintenance depot. The former booking office and waiting room has also survived although the projecting canopy has gone. Not far away is the Manifold Valley Hotel where many old railway pictures are displayed. Once called the Light Railway Hotel, it was one of three which was NSR owned.

The 2 ft 6 in single track railway, nearly nine miles in length, had its official opening on Monday, 27th June 1904. As already mentioned, the rail link between Leek and Waterhouses came later in July 1905 and local residents, well aware of this delay, organised a large sign to be included in the celebrations reading 'Hurry up North Stafford'. The opening ceremony for the L&MVLR was carried out by the Earl of Dartmouth, Lord Lieutenant of the County of Stafford, after which a train, comprising two carriages and two trucks fitted with temporary seats, took Lord Dartmouth and the invited guests on 'an exceedingly pleasant journey'.

The L&MVLR possessed just two locomotives during its existence. Both 2-6-4Ts, built by Kitson & Co in 1904, they were nos 1 and 2, named *E R Calthrop* and *J B Earle* purchased for £1,725 each. Four tramway-type bogie coaches were used, each with a length of 42 feet. Perhaps most surprising was the fact that 8 ft wide coaches were used on a 2 ft 6 in gauge track and, in order to do this, special agreement had to be given by the Board of Trade. The coaches had colonial-type end platforms and were fitted with large side windows so that passengers could enjoy the delightful scenery along the valley.

Unhappily the L&MVLR was never able to build up any worthwhile freight business and, with almost total reliance on passenger traffic, it could not survive indefinitely and finances suffered. A proposed extension to Buxton might have saved the day but this was opposed by the NSR as well as local landowners. The LNWR were equally disinterested and the scheme which had lingered for many years had to be dropped. Equally a proposal from the L&MVLR directors that the NSR should purchase the line proved unsuccessful. For a time during the First World War, the line played an important role with the carriage of large quantities of milk in 17 gallon churns.

After the war the line suffered along with others from coal and railway strikes and the increase in competition from road transport. In January 1923 both the NSR and the L&MVLR became part of the London, Midland & Scottish Railway (LMS) following 'grouping' of railway companies into four main areas. Yet despite seasonal tourist traffic, the LMS had little interest in this comparatively unknown route. With the line losing money, the LMS announced that services would end on Monday, 12th March 1934.

The last train ran on Saturday, 10th March, with few supporters turning up for a final ride. The weather was cold and misty with both Leek and Waterhouses under 3 inches of snow. Within a few years, the locomotives and coaches had been scrapped and the

A mixed train in the Manifold Valley c1905. The first two wagons are on a special transporter used for carrying standard gauge stock. (Lens of Sutton)

The former booking office and waiting room of the Leek & Manifold Valley Light Railway at Hulme End in May 1992. The projecting canopy has been removed. (Author)

track lifted. The only saving grace was the purchase of the trackbed and bridges by Staffordshire County Council, which spent £6,000 in converting the route into a footpath and bridleway. At least in such a way, visitors could continue to enjoy the delights of the beautiful Manifold Valley. What a terrible shame the line did not last until enthusiasts might have acquired it to provide a preserved railway. Today it could hardly fail.

Chapter 17

A GNR LINE ACROSS STAFFORDSHIRE

(Stafford/Chartley/Uttoxeter)

In the early days of the Stafford & Uttoxeter Railway (S&UR) there were often difficulties over connections with London & North Western Railway (LNWR) trains at Stafford. To overcome this, the S&UR trains had to frequently increase speed when running late and it was such an instance that caused a bad accident in May 1868. A train was already behind time when leaving Uttoxeter and so the engine crew took Hopton Bank just prior to Stafford too fast. As a result the train was derailed on a curve at the end of the cutting.

Two crew members were killed, two were seriously injured and eight passengers were also hurt. In the book *The Stafford & Uttoxeter Railway*, P. Jones wrote that a report to the Board of Trade stated that the track might have been slightly 'out of gauge' due to heavy frost and the weight of the leading pair of locomotive's wheels was not enough to hold them down. The S&UR argued that since the LNWR refused to wait for connections, trains had to be driven hard especially if passengers travelling onward to Shrewsbury were aboard.

There was a further serious accident in March 1882 when a special train travelling from Derby was derailed at Chartley. Stirl-

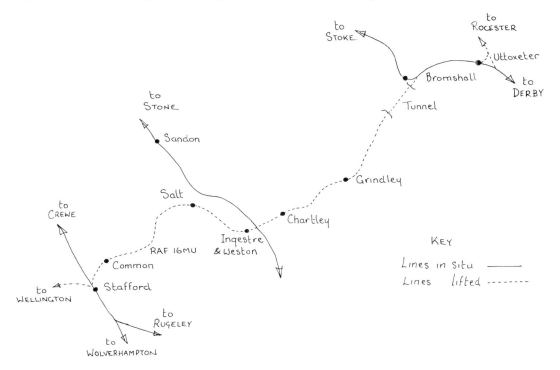

KEY

Lines in situ ——————
Lines lifted ----------

NSR locomotive no 40 2-4-2T class A hauling a passenger set waits at Uttoxeter station c1910. The line to the left came from Rocester and closed in January 1965 (Lens of Sutton)

ing locomotive 0-4-2 no 569 was hauling three coaches, 13 horse boxes and a brake van plus further horse boxes, these last being without proper vacuum brake control. Because of this the driver was advised to proceed with caution but, unaware that a passing loop had just been brought into use at Chartley, the driver entered the station too fast causing a derailment.

All the horse boxes struck the platform, several horses were killed or injured and many vehicles broke up. No passengers were hurt, only shaken. Following the accident, it was recommended that all future passing loops should be built with facing points on the straight. Chartley's layout was altered accordingly and a 10 mph speed limit was introduced.

The Stafford and Uttoxeter Railway, known locally as the 'Clog and Knocker', was agreed by Parliament in July 1862. Construction was difficult with the need for a tunnel at Bromshall (321 yards) and also a cutting at Hopton where blasting through solid rock was necessary. The line opened on 23rd December 1867 and intermediate stations were built at Salt (known as Salt & Sandon after 1904), Ingestre & Weston, Stowe (renamed Chartley in 1874) and Grindley. Within the Act, a branch of almost two miles to Weston on the NSR had also been agreed and, subsequently, another to Abbot's Bromley to the south. Neither of these two additions were ever built.

Perhaps an explanation as to why the Stafford to Uttoxeter Railway was built at all was that the Great Northern Railway (GNR), which worked the line from the start, hoped to provide a link between Central Wales and Uttoxeter and then on to the Nottinghamshire/Derbyshire coalfields. Such plans had been strongly opposed by the LNWR and the NSR with the result that only a stretch between Stafford and Bromshall junction was ever completed. To reach Uttoxeter from Bromshall junction, trains had to run on NSR tracks.

In July 1874, a further station opened known as The Common (later known as Stafford Common) to cater for a growing popula-

A train hauled by GNR locomotive no 23 leaves Uttoxeter for Stafford c1910. The line opened in December 1867 and passenger services lasted just over 70 years. (Lens of Sutton)

tion to the north of Stafford and also for passengers travelling to the nearby horse racing. Meanwhile the S&UR was running into financial difficulties and in 1879 a Bill allowed the GNR to use its tracks. This meant that, in addition, the GNR would use the section of NSR track from Bromshall junction to Uttoxeter so in return it was agreed that the NSR could use S&UR lines. Traffic on the line increased but the S&UR had virtually lost its independence and, two years later in 1881, the GNR purchased the S&UR for £100,000.

With wider scope now possible, a service between Stafford and Derby commenced in November 1881 which connected with Nottingham, Grantham and Burton. The GNR took every opportunity to exploit its line including the provision of many excursion trains to East Coast resorts. Early GNR locomotives seen on the line included class E2 2-4-0s built by Stirling at Doncaster in 1882, renowned for their 6 ft 7 in driving wheels. Soon after the turn of the century a Stirling class 0-6-0 was introduced.

Salt production had long been a feature in parts of Staffordshire,

Only two bare platforms and bus-stop type shelters exist today at Uttoxeter for a service between Stoke and Derby. The former line branching away to Rocester has become a car park. (Author)

discovered in the Common area during water boring. It was not until around the turn of the century that a company established itself in this area to the south of the line with further companies soon to follow. By 1913 over 81,000 tons of salt were being produced annually.

When war broke out in September 1939, the line was reduced to one train each way daily. On 4th December 1939, regular passenger services were completely withdrawn but the line acquired a new importance. An RAF Maintenance Unit was established not far from Stafford Common and in addition an army depot was set up at Bromshall, both with numerous sidings. The purpose of the RAF unit was to serve as a maintenance and supplies depot for RAF planes and equipment and a complex track layout was constructed.

The Air Ministry sidings remained busy after the war as overseas bases were wound down and equipment was returned for storage or disposal. At nationalisation in 1948, the line between Bromshall junction and the Air Ministry sidings closed, yet some nine years later, on 23rd March 1957, many enthusiasts were able to enjoy a 'last ride' on the branch. The Stephenson Locomotive Society (Midlands area) organised a three coach push-pull set hauled by Ivatt 2-6-2T no 41224 to travel the line.

A journey along the former route today reveals a few reminders of the past. At Stafford the bay that once housed Uttoxeter trains has become a car park. The station and trackbed at Salt have gone but the station-master's house has become a private residence. At

All that remains at Salt, an intermediate station on the Stafford/Uttoxeter line, is the station-master's house, today a private residence. The track and platform have long since gone. (Author)

Stafford station, platforms 3 & 4, in the 1960s. The bay on the far right that served Uttoxeter trains has gone, having become a car park. The coal hopper on the left has also been removed.(Lens of Sutton)

Grindley, the road bridge and embankments can still be found. Uttoxeter is a pale shadow of its former self. Gone are the platform awnings, the footbridge, the sidings, the tall semaphore signals and the signal boxes. The line which swung northwards towards Rocester has also gone with the former platform area partly replaced by a car park completed in the late 1980s. The two remaining platforms appear bare and uninviting with their 'bus-stop' type shelters serving the few trains that ply daily between Stoke and Derby.

Chapter 18

LOST LINES FROM WALSALL AND THE 'TUTBURY JENNIE'

(Walsall/Cannock/Rugeley, Walsall/Brownhills/Lichfield/
Wichnor jct/Burton-on-Trent, Burton-on-Trent/Tutbury)

Walsall/Cannock/Rugeley

When trains reached Cannock from Walsall on 1st February 1858, Cannock was 'the end of the line'. Any travel across the Chase to the Trent Valley at Rugeley was laborious indeed requiring a trek over rough roads. With coal being brought into production in the Hednesford area this state of affairs did not last long for the coal had to be marketed and a link with the industrial Midlands was needed. Hundreds of navvies were soon at work, building embankments and cutting through gravel and soft sandstone to reach the London & North Western (LNWR) main line at Rugeley (Trent Valley). The Cannock/Rugeley line which opened on 7th November 1859 was called the Cannock Mineral Railway and was worked by the LNWR. Ten years later, despite competition from the NSR, the LNWR took over the company.

Walsall station c1910 when station-masters wore top hats. The waiting locomotive is an LNWR 0-6-0 originally designed by J Ramsbottom and further developed by F W Webb when it became a 'Special DX6' class. (Lens of Sutton)

The many mineral sidings feeding the Walsall-Rugeley line provided the route with much of its traffic. Trucks came to Hednesford from collieries such as West Cannock, Brereton or Cannock Wood where they were marshalled into trains before starting out for destinations via Rugeley or Walsall. Miners were carried to and from the pits in what were known as 'Paddy' trains which had wooden seats. These were necessary because in earlier times there were no pithead baths. The last of these ran in the early 1920s with many men changing to buses which ran directly to and from the pitheads.

Moors Gorse Halt between Hednesford and Rugeley became

Staff at Cannock station c1905. Trains first reached Cannock in 1858 which served as a terminus until the line was completed the following year to the LNWR main line at Rugeley. (Photograph courtesy Cannock library)

A steam railcar approaches Hednesford c1910. The line closed to passenger traffic in January 1965 but re-opened in April 1989 between Walsall and Hednesford with the prospect of reaching Rugeley and providing a through service to Stafford. (Photograph courtesy Cannock library)

well known to many RAF servicemen during the Second World War when a camp was sited on nearby Brindley Heath. The lane from the halt leading up to the camp became affectionately known as 'Kitbag Hill'. After the war, traffic between Walsall and Rugeley dwindled but it was not until 18th January 1965 that the line closed to passenger traffic although freight traffic continued.

Almost a quarter of a century later on 7th April 1989 the line re-opened from Walsall to Hednesford recognising a need for commuter passenger traffic. There are plans that the Hednesford to Rugeley section will follow thus providing a through service to Stafford. Diesel units carry passengers today – a far cry from the 'Paddy' trains of yesteryear.

Walsall/Brownhills/Lichfield/Wichnor jct/Burton-on-Trent
The South Staffordshire Railway (SSR) opened a line from Walsall to Wichnor junction on 9th April 1849 where it joined the main Midland Railway route to Burton-on-Trent over which it had

Hednesford station, May 1992, re-opened in April 1989. The original platform buildings were demolished partly because of damage from subsidence caused by the nearby pits. (Author)

running powers. Intermediate stations opened at Rushall, Pelsall, Brownhills, Hammerwich and Lichfield. A station at Trent Valley Junction where the branch crossed the main line between Rugeley and Tamworth followed later in August.

The line was in a way unique for, following disagreements within the SSR board, Parliament agreed the line could be leased to an individual, John McClean, for the unusually long period of 21 years. McClean was no newcomer to railways having previously served as engineer to the broad gauge line constructed between Wolverhampton and Birmingham.

Rugeley station on the main LNWR line from Lichfield to Stafford. The nameboard read, 'Rugeley. Junction for Hednesford, Cannock and Walsall'. The platform buildings and canopy have long since gone. (Lens of Sutton)

When McClean gave up his lease in 1861, ten years before expiry, the SSR transferred to the LNWR. This caused problems over the running rights previously enjoyed by the SSR from Wichnor junction to Burton-on-Trent. The Midland Railway was not happy about the LNWR using its tracks and battles followed. Midland Railway men considered they treated their own engines with feeling and, as one Midland driver claimed, 'not like the

rough and ready LNWR men who did dreadful things to their engines in the interests of speed, economy and punctuality'. The Midland Railway claimed comfort and cleanliness as priorities and considered that the trains the LNWR brought into Burton, often hauled by 'Cauliflower' 0-6-0 engines, were 'coal black and unkempt'.

The Midland Railway soon gave way and it is recorded that on the day in question an LNWR locomotive made 'a triumphal journey towards Burton'. Goods trains to Burton and later to Derby soon became regular traffic and in addition an LNWR goods depot was established at Burton station. Yet rivalry between LNWR and Midland drivers continued for many years, even after 'grouping' in the 1920s. It is recorded that a former Midland driver, relaxing in his garden one summer evening, heard a locomotive with wheels slipping on a gradient and smoke billowing over him from what was previously an LNWR line. He was heard to comment, 'B__ ____y North Western Man'!

The Walsall to Wichnor junction line closed to passenger traffic on 18th January 1965, the same day as the Walsall to Rugeley branch. Yet the area is not without its reminders of the past. The Chasewater Light Railway, founded in 1959, operates a section of track in Chasewater Pleasure Park, the stretch once part of a Midland Railway spur into the Cannock Chase coalfield. Here many industrial tank locomotives can be seen and steam rides alongside the lake can be enjoyed.

A more up-to-date reminder perhaps came about with the re-opening of the former line between Lichfield Town and Lichfield Trent Valley in October 1989. This had made possible the use of BR's new class 323 4-coach units which provide a regular passenger service between Birmingham New Street and Lichfield TV, the latter connecting with the main Birmingham-avoiding Intercity line.

Rugeley station May 1992. The station buildings have long since gone with the present windswept platforms hardly resembling their former selves. (Author)

119

A Midland Railway passenger train with non-corridor stocks waits at Burton-on-Trent as viewed from the station bridge. The station buildings seen here were demolished in the early 1970s. (Lens of Sutton)

Burton-on-Trent/Tutbury

Visit Horninglow, a few miles out of Burton-on-Trent, and the Jennie Inn can be found close to where trains once stopped at an intermediate station on their journey between Burton and Tutbury. The line no longer exists and the pub is one of the few reminders. Despite this the 'Tutbury Jennie', as it was known, is still remembered with affection by many local residents. Burton to Tutbury and back, 5½ miles each way, was a passenger service which began on 11th September 1848 and lasted well over a century. In its earliest days the line was run by the North Staffordshire Railway (NSR) and after 'grouping' by the London, Midland & Scottish Railway (LMS).

The line to Tutbury was one of Burton's least important, for at the turn of the century around 150 main line passenger trains either left or called at the station each day. Burton's original station was completed in 1839 following the opening of the Birmingham & Derby Junction Railway. The station was rebuilt in 1883 at the same time as Station Bridge which crosses over the tracks. Burton station became well known as a place where lunch or tea baskets could be ordered in advance and taken to the train by attendants. For 3/3d (about 18p) a basket comprised a chop or steak with vegetables, cheese, butter, fruit etc., plus a bottle of beer or wine. When so-called modernisation came in 1971 Burton station lost its buildings, canopy and its fine wrought-iron work.

The 'Tutbury Jennie' usually comprised a small tank locomotive and one, two or three non-corridor coaches. Later 'push-pull' motor trains were introduced avoiding the need for the engine to

120

change ends. Intermediate stations were at Horninglow, Stretton & Clay Mills and Rolleston-on-Dove but all these closed on 1st January 1949. The service carried on until 11th June 1960 when local people turned out in force to bid farewell to a much loved line. The locomotive was a 1950 Crewe built 2-6-2T no 41277 and on its last run back to Burton there were some 500 people in the three coaches. To add to the merriment one passenger blew a bugle during the whole journey.

Tutbury station c1910 on the North Staffordshire Railway between Derby and Uttoxeter. The station was also the terminus for the 'Tutbury Jennie' from Burton-on-Trent. (Lens of Sutton)

CONCLUSION

The decline of many branches began in the 1920s. Buses were able to offer a more flexible service than the trains and road haulage was on the increase. In addition the private motor car was beginning to make its presence felt. After nationalisation in 1948, the railways, still recovering from the demands of war service, were slow to meet any competition and were losing ground. Reduced revenue was leading to increased economies and then closures, with the entire pattern of inland transport gradually changing.

An early closure in Shropshire was the short branch from Lightmoor to Shifnal on the main Shrewsbury to Wolverhampton line which ceased passenger traffic in September 1925. In Staffordshire the Biddulph Valley line from Stoke to Congleton was an early casualty closing in July 1927 when the LMS considered the line had no future for passenger traffic. In the early 1930s other lines quickly followed including the branches from Harecastle, northwards to Sandbach and southwards to Keele. In Shropshire the 'Potts' line, as it was known, closed in November 1933. After the Second World War, many more lines came to grief.

In March 1963 proposals were made in a report which became popularly known as the 'Beeching Plan'. Basically the idea was to keep lines considered suitable to rail traffic and give up the remainder. It was claimed that one third of the rail system in Britain carried only 1% of the total traffic! Further drastic cuts inevitably followed and many more lines disappeared. Closures – at first a trickle – became a torrent. Where branches once existed, some linking major routes across the region, soon only the original trunk routes remained. A few branch lines have survived but their future must surely be considered as uncertain.

What of plans for the future in the area? There is encouraging news over plans to re-introduce passenger services between Loughborough, Leicester, Burton-upon-Trent and Derby. An hourly service of Sprinter trains is planned and numerous new stations are proposed. Costs are put at up to £15 million but it is anticipated that up to nearly 2 million passengers might be carried annually. Following a Government grant agreed in early January 1992, Leicester County Council plan to have a service operational in stages in 1994 and 1995. It will become known as *The Ivanhoe Line*, named after Sir Walter Scott's famous novel *Ivanhoe* which was centred on the castle at Ashby de la Zouche.

There has been news too of lines re-opened in the south of Staffordshire. Passenger traffic recommenced between Walsall, Cannock and Hednesford in April 1989 with consideration being given to the extension of this service at a future date to Rugeley on the Trent Valley line. In October 1989 passenger services also restarted between Lichfield City and Lichfield Trent Valley and, with electrification completed, advanced new-style class 323 trains will provide a speedy cross-city service between Redditch and Lichfield.

Such news is however of little comfort to Shropshire travellers where the county town of Shrewsbury has lost its InterCity rail connection with London. Passengers today are relegated to a second-class journey to Wolverhampton where they must change. The majority of travellers in Shropshire are outraged at the decision, well aware that millions are being spent on road improvements at the expense of the railways. To many it is hard to be convinced that the railways, other than the major networks, are not being deliberately run down.

One reversing trend has proved encouraging. Gobowen station on the 1848 Birmingham-Shrewsbury-Chester line, recently de-staffed, has been taken over by schoolgirls from nearby Moreton Hall School. Lower sixth-formers serve as directors, sell tickets, announce trains and have even repainted the booking office and waiting room. Profits go into a fund to re-open another station further down the line – Whittington. BR consider the situation unique – perhaps the trickle of interest will become a torrent thus saving many more stations from extinction.

With the threat of rail privatisation ever present, rural train services are particularly vulnerable, these alone absorbing a large portion of BR's annual subsidy. There has been talk of returning to separate companies thus encouraging competition such as in the days before, or even after 'grouping'. Sadly today's working climate – with ever present redundancies – makes such an idea a mere illusion. It is almost 150 years since railways came to Shropshire and Staffordshire. What a downhill path many lines have taken since the days of the Great Western or the London, Midland & Scottish Railways – or, even earlier, since the proud days of the 'Knotty'.

OPENING AND FINAL CLOSURE DATES OF LINES TO REGULAR PASSENGER TRAFFIC

Line	Opened	Final Closure
Burton-on-Trent/Tutbury	11 Sep 1848	13 June 1960
Walsall/Brownhills/Lichfield/ Wichnor jct	9 Apr 1849	18 Jan 1965*[1]
Wellington/Newport/Stafford	1 June 1849	7 Sep 1964
Uttoxeter/Leek/North Rode	13 Jul 1849	4 Jan 1965
Rocester/Ashbourne	31 May 1852	1 Nov 1954*[2]
Walsall/Cannock	1 Feb 1858	18 Jan 1965*[3]
Wellington/Horsehay Ironworks	2 May 1859	23 Jul 1962
Cannock/Hednesford/Rugeley	7 Nov 1859	18 Jan 1965*[3]
Oswestry/Welshpool	14 Aug 1860	18 Jan 1965
Shrewsbury/Pontesbury/ Minsterley	14 Feb 1861	5 Feb 1951
Wellington/Oakengates/ Coalport (East)	17 Jun 1861	2 Jun 1952
Horsehay Ironworks/ Lightmoor	1 Aug 1861	23 Jul 1962
Lightmoor/Shifnal	1 Aug 1861	21 Sep 1925*[4]
Woofferton/Tenbury Wells	1 Aug 1861	31 Jul 1961
Shrewsbury/Coalport/ Bridgnorth/Bewdley	1 Feb 1862	9 Sep 1963*[5]
Bewdley/Hartlebury	1 Feb 1862	5 Jan 1970
Buildwas/Much Wenlock	1 Feb 1862	23 Jul 1962
Stoke/Silverdale	7 Apr 1862	2 Mar 1964
Llanymynech/Llanfyllin	17 Jul 1863	18 Jan 1965
Market Drayton/Nantwich	20 Oct 1863	9 Sep 1963
Stoke/Bucknall/Congleton	1 Jun 1864	11 Jul 1927
Oswestry/Whitchurch	27 Jul 1864	18 Jan 1965
Tenbury Wells/Bewdley	13 Aug 1864	1 Aug 1962
Ludlow/Bitterley	24 Aug 1864	31 Dec 1962
Buildwas/Lightmoor	1 Nov 1864	23 Jul 1962
Much Wenlock/Presthope	5 Dec 1864	31 Dec 1951
Craven Arms/Stretford Bridge/Lydham Heath/ Bishop's Castle	1 Feb 1866	20 Apr 1935
Shrewsbury/Kinnerley/ Llanymynech	13 Aug 1866	6 Nov 1933*[6]
Bitterley/Clee Hill	1 Jun 1867	7 Nov 1960
Wellington/Market Drayton	16 Oct 1867	9 Sep 1963
Bucknall/Endon/Leek	1 Nov 1867	7 May 1956
Presthope/Craven Arms	16 Dec 1867	31 Dec 1951
Stafford/Chartley/Uttoxeter	23 Dec 1867	4 Dec 1939

Silverdale/Market Drayton	1 Feb 1870	5 May 1956
Llanymynech/Nantmawr	18 Apr 1870	1 Jan 1917
Kinnerley/Criggion	2 Jun 1871	6 Nov 1933
Etruria/Tunstall/Kidsgrove	15 Nov 1875	2 Mar 1964
Pontesbury/Snailbeach	Jul 1877	1959
Bewdley/Kidderminster	1 Jun 1878	3 Jan 1970
Keele/Audley/Harecastle	28 Jun 1880	27 Apr 1931
Harecastle/Sandbach	3 Jul 1893	28 Jul 1930
Ellesmere/Wrexham	2 Nov 1895	10 Sep 1962
Cresswell/Cheadle	1 Jan 1901	17 Jun 1963
Porthywaen/Llangynog (Tanat Valley)	5 Jan 1904	5 Feb 1951
Waterhouses/Hulme End	27 Jun 1904	12 Mar 1934
Leek/Waterhouses	1 Jul 1905	30 Sep 1935
Cleobury Mortimer/Ditton Priors	21 Nov 1908	26 Sep 1938
Trentham/Trentham Park	1 Apr 1910	1 Oct 1957

*[1]Lichfield City to Lichfield Trent Valley re-opened to passenger traffic, October 1989

*[2]Emergency winter services continued between Rocester and Ashbourne for a number of years after official closure

*[3]Line connecting Walsall, Cannock and Hednesford re-opened to passenger traffic, April 1989.

*[4]Shifnal to Lightmoor branch closed to passengers from March 1915 to July 1925. Line finally closed to passengers 21st September 1925.

*[5]Steam trains recommenced at Bridgnorth on May 23rd 1970 when the Severn Valley Railway Society started limited services. Services from Bridgnorth to Kidderminster started on July 30th 1984.

*[6]Shrewsbury to Llanymynech re-opened by War Department during World War II. Final closure 29th Feb 1960

INDEX